Luck

Luck

Margaret Randall

Drawings by **Barbara Byers**

New Village Press • New York

Published in the United States by New Village Press
bookorders@newvillagepress.net
www.newvillagepress.org
New Village Press is a public-benefit, nonprofit publisher
Distributed by NYU Press

Paperback ISBN 978-1-61332-219-2
Hardcover ISBN 978-1-61332-220-8
eBook Trade ISBN 978-1-61332-221-5
eBook Institutional ISBN 978-1-61332-222-2

Library of Congress Control Number: 2023942281

*This book is for Greg Smith, Rich Gabriel
and all those who keep doing the work.*

Contents

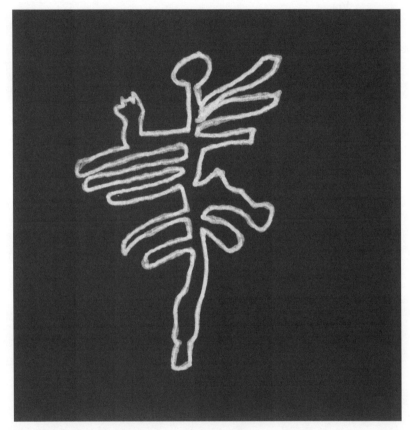

Figure 1

Seasons

Winter tries its best to erase our shame. She curls about us, cold pretending to be heat and filling our lungs with glacial air. Every year we appreciate her effort, applaud her persistence, take comfort from how hard she tries. If we pay attention, we discover that winter traces new boundaries across our maps, insidious lines that would divide us from ourselves. But if we have the courage to walk those borderlands, we discover *Nepantla*, a liminal space where we may hide our exhaustion in mountains of exuberance, rough oceans of memory, great open spaces filled with passion, forests where ancient trees embrace forgotten histories, deserts where we may undress and give ourselves to time.

All our lives we've had to learn to look winter in the eye, breathe her in, teach her that we have the stamina to confront her perils. Those who accompany us on winter's shores become ghosts as we watch them fade from view. We reach out to touch them and our hands fall back empty, disconcerted. We are forced to chase their disappearing footsteps: season to season, year to year. No one told us that winter struggles with such jealous rage. Only her thick makeup gives her pain away.

Spring calls herself renewal, takes pride in the designation. Why should we require a new garden to remind us of what we already know? If we play the waiting game and win, summer will come. But it's never that easy. Sometimes where we expect a flower to unfurl its petals, a tree to hang heavy with fruit, or tomatoes to appear red and inviting on the vine, all that litters the ground about us are stunted ears of corn vanquished by chemical madness, oversized melons hollowed in bitterness, potatoes rotting in the earth, fruit half-devoured by starving birds and insects.

Spring bursts with dazzle and relief but beware: not everything is what it seems. Some promises remain in the design stage, advertising more than they can deliver. What we fail to understand, year after year, is that effort is also required of us. Only symbiosis and teamwork model a future of plenty.

Summer is the prize. But she only shines while still carrying the scent of spring. It is a cooperative time, dependent on legacy to sound a harmonious song. I lie naked in the sun, mindful of how my body has changed through the years. From tender baby chubbiness, caressed but frightened . . . to the young woman focused on what never mattered and unaware of what did . . . to the fullness of motherhood and perfect pleasure of maturity crouching low in bountiful nests of graying hair . . . and finally, to this skeletal wheeze bearing the dark blotches of too much sun and work.

Summer tries to console and sometimes does. But, despite her best intentions, she is drowning in nostalgia, an imposter vying for stardom and forced to make do with the understudy role. Perhaps one day, long after she is gone, we will look at her creations and be inspired to make our art of the future.

Because it challenges our deepest thirsts and desires, autumn is my favorite season. She fights hard to hold onto weather, keep her temperatures in check. She engages in serious games with tangible consequences, gives her all and is always willing to take another chance. She never lies and we always know where we stand when embraced by her shadow. Her calendar displays the darkest days and also those that keep us alive. October is her most powerful month. Its heart thunders in my breast, signaling risk, overpowering all reluctant voices.

Some latitudes paint the seasons vigorously. Others, closer to the equator, are lazy and only small variations in heat or cold announce their passage from one to another.

We are taught that the year begins in January's desire, that the winds of March are dangerous to our species, that June is a month of beginnings, and that August, the coyote, will always try to trick us. December's jubilation eventually abandons whimsy, and on midnight of its 31st day a blank page falls expectant in our laps. Then the cycle begins again.

Until now, we have taken our medicine obediently, eager to keep memory at bay as one season passes to the next. But today is different. Today we will refuse its numbing manipulation.

Today is the day we take note of where and when we are.

Naked

A s in *without clothes*? No, I'm thinking of a much more dramatic
nakedness, one in which nine decades of secrets are laid bare in all
their complicated sordidness and surprise. What filled my mother's mind
as she succumbed to the anesthesia and long metal prongs grasped my
shoulders, dragging me from between her legs. My first breath, opening
my eyes and looking around. What sensations and emotions swam in my
head, unintelligible to those around me?

Childhood lies. Crouching beneath the stairs in the Scarsdale house,
conversing with my four imaginary friends. Those talks we had, the ones
that nurtured me when adults avoided my questions. The things those
invented friends told me. The things I remember. What I couldn't ask back
then but later brought me up short with their eloquence.

Teenage lies. The stories I invented when I followed my carefully tended
Geological Survey maps across desert rises and hollows, found a flat rock,
undressed, and spent edgy nights imagining myself a woman on that land
before the Conquest broke it. All the unwritten stories. What I said to the
boys who wanted to kiss me in parked cars. What I told my girlfriends and
parents about those encounters.

What my first mentors told me. And what I made of their gifts.

My fake orgasms and then the real ones. Joy and anguish, first with men and then the woman I have loved almost four decades now. What we create together. The words I screamed in effort as I gave birth to Gregory, Sarah, Ximena, and Ana. Moans of pain settling into to the purr of motherhood.

The lies I told the enemy—by commission or omission—because I was a David to its Goliath and believed anything was justified in that unequal battle. The truth I told myself when I learned to ask questions and demand answers and finally understood that the victory we needed depended on the way we reached our goal as much as on having arrived.

How I came to understand the struggles we waged, and especially our defeats. The pride I retain in the wake of failure. The fullness of knowing it couldn't have been otherwise. We didn't win, but we had to try. And there was honor and power in the trying. Integrity and dignity are qualities that matter.

How everything came clear when I understood the place art has in our lives. What it means. The language it speaks. How it changes everything else, its importance to our survival. And above all, how it carries us to a place beyond the give and take of success or defeat. How all the pieces fall into place again and then again if I am able to see my art in that context, my poems written upon that map.

I have recognized so much of what I now hold in my head in just these past few torturous years. Fascism, evangelical condescension, bull-headed ignorance, a refusal to care for this planet we inhabit and the inevitable realization that we are using it up, are tragic yet impressive teachers. Once we prided ourselves in what we were creating for our children and their children. Now we know we will leave another, sadder, legacy. The tragedy of loss.

People, experience, and memory have created such a detailed cartography in my brain, so many raging synapses and delights of connection, that the composite often leaks without warning, causing a flashflood that may seem dangerous to others. I take a breath and keep on talking. And listening.

Age brings its own nakedness. If I physically disrobe, all you will see is shriveled flesh, a spread of liver spots, flaccid breasts hanging like diminished pouches with vague memories of the sustenance they once gave, the connections they established, a pubis as hairless and smooth as a baby's but with a dimming history, and windows of pink among tufts of white dotting my head. But if could bare what lives in my mind, all the pleadings and declarations, all the ideas and memories and images from so many years of living, my nakedness might blind the world.

No doomsday would be able to dim its light.

9/11

Certain events are so catastrophic, joyous, or otherwise meaningful that they are forever after known by their date alone. For centuries in the United States the second Monday in October has been called Columbus Day, honoring the arrival of Christopher Columbus, the Italian explorer who accidentally landed on the shores of a New World: the moment from which we date the European conquest of the Americas. In recent times, many have renamed the date *Indigenous People's Day*, shifting the focus from conqueror to conquered. The name-change promotes consciousness, but the suffering of native peoples at the hands of those who stole their lands and resources continues. African Americans rarely point to a single date that recalls their ancestors having been kidnapped and brought to this country in slave ships; the Middle Passage, as it is called, took place from 1700 to roughly 1808: not one day but more than one hundred years of dislocation and death.

July 4, 1776, was the day the Second Continental Congress unanimously adopted our Constitution, officially separating the United States from Great Britain. The Fourth of July today is experienced as hotdogs and potato salad, fireworks exploding against a complacent sky. November 9, 1799, was the day the French revolution ended, the world's first win for liberal democracy. October 25, 1917, marks the victory of the Russian revolution, the world's earliest socialist insurrection. On May 7, 1945, the United States, England, France, and their allies triumphed over Germany and Italy. Since then, the following day, May 8th, has been celebrated as the date European fascism was defeated. The importance of the holiday reflected our emotion at having secured freedom over barbary. Little did we know that even within our lifetimes fascism under other names would once again gain power in so many parts of the world. August 6th and 9th commemorate the first atomic bombs dropped by the United States on the Japanese cities of Hiroshima and Nagasaki, the first weapons of mass destruction used by any nation against another. The official US story is that the vile attacks put an end to World War II and saved hundreds of thousands of lives. The Japanese mourn their more than 200,000 dead and maimed and warn against similar criminality.

December 25th marks the Christian holiday of Christmas, while in 2022 the Jewish Rosh Hashanah was September 26–27, and in 2023 Muslim Eid al-Adha took place June 28–29. Some dates follow alternative calendric progressions or are moveable feasts because they depend upon yearly events that change with the harvest or other important moments.

When people in the United States hear the date 9/11, we automatically think of the coordinated airline hijackings and suicide attacks perpetrated by nineteen militants of the Islamic extremist group al-Qaeda against New York City's Twin Towers, the Pentagon in Washington, and a field in Pennsylvania where one of the three planes was forced down by its passengers on September 11, 2001. Almost 3,000 people died at the combined sites. Ninth month of the year, eleventh day: shorthand for the worst terrorist attack on US soil.

Yet the date holds other meanings that have been opaqued and, in many cases, entirely erased by those four weaponized planes. If you google the date, you'll find more than one hundred historic events that have happened on that day. Random among them are the following: In 1565, the Ottoman forces retreated, ending the Great Siege of Malta. In 1775,

Benedict Arnold's expedition to Quebec left Cambridge, Massachusetts. In 1857, the Mountain Meadows Massacre took place: Mormons disguised as Paiutes attacked settlers, resulting in 120 dead. In 1919, the United States Marine Corps invaded Honduras, one of many such US military forays in Latin America. In 1972, the San Francisco Bay Area Rapid Transit system began passenger service. In 1997, NASA's Mars Global Surveyor reached Mars. And in 2007, Russia tested the largest conventional weapon ever, dubbed the Father of All Bombs.

Most importantly to many of my generation, on September 11, 1973, a military coup ousted the democratically elected Popular Unity government in Chile, ending a socialist experiment achieved at the polls, causing President Salvador Allende to take his own life, and initiating a period of terror and torture lasting for almost two decades. Before 2001, to anyone who cared about recent Latin American history, if you mentioned 9/11 you were referring to Pinochet's coup. After that year, by virtue of its global dominance, the United States usurped the date.

I remember my shock as I watched the repeated television images of those planes flying into the buildings, huge billows of black smoke issuing from them, the horror of human bodies falling eighty or one hundred stories to the pavement below, and the eventual collapse of the structures themselves. As that long day ended, my wife Barbara and I sought community where we might come together in collective pain. We walked to our nearby university campus. A circle of likeminded people had already gathered and one after another began to speak. When someone pontificated that *the chickens have come home to roost*, we walked away, deeply troubled by such a simplistic and arrogant description of a tragedy that had taken so many lives.

Yes, the United States has a history of invading other countries. Yes, imperialism, colonialism, and racism have characterized us for centuries. Yes, the 9/11 attack was meant as payback; all that was clear. But the use of that flippant characterization of what had been perpetrated struck us as ignorant and uncaring. Some three thousand families were grieving their loved ones. Innocent Arab Americans (or anyone who looked like an Arab American) would undoubtedly be the targets of racist violence. Our response called for compassion and then some analysis of why and how the attacks happened, not a glib slogan that rode roughshod over tragedy. Over the following two decades, a dumbed down and dangerous response by both government and ordinary people would show just how counter-productive such rhetoric is.

History is told by the victors. Dates are inscribed on calendars accord-ing to what those who write the histories want future generations to remember. The same date may memorialize a win for some and unspeak-able loss for others. Likewise, great fanfare around a particular event may erase another that took place on the same day somewhere else. This is what happened here in the United States, to the Chilean tragedy, and to anything else that happened on any September 11th throughout known history any-where in the world.

Horrendous as it was, when we in the United States refer to Septem-ber 11, 2001, as 9/11, we are speaking *Americanese*, a language only under-stood by those who ignore or disparage other peoples' histories and cultures. We are recolonizing colonization. Extreme nationalism tends to engrave certain dates on humanity's calendar, leaving others off or surrendering them only to those who have suffered or profited directly.

Figure 2

Anger

The thing about anger is that it can consume you, literally destroy your body and mind. It may corrode your organs and your breath, burst forth at inappropriate moments, devastate you without even touching those who provoke it. We must avoid using it irresponsibly, save it for the times when it is warranted.

The language of anger is difficult to learn. It's many accents may confuse.

A look at anger's contrasting behaviors goes a long way toward describing how it can manifest itself. This story comes from men's professional tennis. Arthur Asch was a black man born and raised in Richmond, Virginia, heart of the US American South. He played in streets adorned with statues honoring those who had tried to destroy his people. The lynching of black men was common throughout his youth. He had to measure every glance and temper every verbal expression. He was forced to hide his anger beneath a calm exterior as the racist society in which he lived threatened his life daily. The slightest relinquishment of control could have gotten him killed. Despite the many obstacles in his way, he became the world's best player in a game that was 99 percent white.

John McEnroe was a younger tennis great, white, and privileged. Each man, in his time, rose to the top of the sport. McEnroe was famous for calling out judges when they issued decisions that he considered to be unfair. He gestured wildly, spewed invectives, and was known to throw his expensive racket onto the court, smashing it to pieces. He performed his anger.

Ashe's anger was invisible to others; he had grown up knowing he must not let it loose. It was just as real as McEnroe's, just as passionate and infinitely better directed, but invisible as he played at all-white country clubs and enjoyed the respect denied most of those of his race. Vocal leaders in the Civil Rights movement berated him for not using his position as a platform for justice. As he achieved the fame that made it possible for him to speak out, he began to articulate what had been smoldering in him his entire life. And he did so with a power and eloquence that changed forever what had been a lily-white game. One Black Panther leader who had criticized his early silence later praised him, saying he'd modeled people's right to choose their conduct at their own tempo.

Anger, compressed, correctly aimed, and measured, can be a fuel like no other.

I have been angry in a great many contexts. When I'm faced with injustice and ignorance. When I believe myself or others to be wronged. When I hear people say that art is inspiration and discipline is irrelevant. When selfishness stands in the way of solidarity.

Before I learned to control my anger, I misdirected it, occasionally against those I loved most dearly. Once, only once, I lashed out at one of my children, slapping her repeatedly as she looked at me in bewilderment and hurt. On another occasion I threw a small rocking chair across a room with the force of frustration that all but paralyzed those witnessing the act. The man who dominated my life at the time made a more rational expression impossible. Then I turned my anger inward, and the shock of those rampages required a long period of healing. They are among my most painful memories. Today I reserve my anger for situations and individuals deserving of its passion.

I am angry at war and at those who propel us into it.

I am angry at the lies they tell and unreal outcomes they predict in an attempt to justify their actions.

I am angry at people in power who know they must change their behavior to preserve the earth and its resources but pretend their actions are not to blame because they keep them in luxury toys and second homes.

I am angry at those who cause poverty and homelessness and try to convince us such conditions happen only to those who are lazy or unwilling to work.

I am angry at bigotry in all its forms, and those who belittle and attack those different from themselves.

I am angry at those who taunt and bully anyone, gaining a false sense of superiority at the expense of the vulnerable.

I am angry at corporations that wantonly diminish our resources and then urge us to individually *do our part*, as if solving the problem is our responsibility.

I am angry at an ex-president who made fascism fashionable for almost half our nation.

I am angry at every elected official, past and present, who uses his or her office for personal gain.

I am angry at six men and women wearing black robes who decided it's their right to determine who can vote, and that women must give birth to unwanted children.

I am angry at those who believe they can dictate who I may and may not love.

I am angry at those pseudo-sophisticates who claim to be feminists while exploiting women.

I am angry with opportunists.

I am angry at fundamentalist religions with their messages of salvation for the faithful, enabling them to control and manipulate millions.

I am angry at those who write history from the viewpoint of the master class and erase our memories as actors in our own lives.

I am angry at those who shame us and feed off our shame.

I am angry at those who belittle art, and pity those who cannot reap its energizing power.

I am angry at powerful nations that invade and occupy those that are smaller and weaker.

I am angry at power itself when it is used to denigrate and kill.

As a woman, I harbor an anger that rose within me from my earliest years growing up in a misogynist society. As a female child I couldn't define or express my feelings of rage when I was told I shouldn't act like the boys, couldn't do what they did, learn what they learned, achieve their successes, or reap their pleasures. I grew up feeling suffocated, drowning in a swamp I couldn't name. When my generation's feminism explained that unequal balance of power, I began to understand my life differently. The anger remained but assumed a new and powerful form. It transformed itself into fuel, driving me into the struggle to change the stakes.

Such anger is a renewable resource, animated by love even as love and the trust that comes with healthy loving make palpable room for its righteousness. Today I choose my battles more carefully but fight with renewed intensity.

Like the atom or neutron, anger in repose is invisible. When set into motion, it displays a brilliance that blinds, a force that can destroy or give birth to a world where it would be superfluous.

The Dream

This was a dream of a different color. By which I mean it was more vivid than others, its areas of contention delineated with thick black lines like a painting by Rouault. Not a nightmare, of which I have many. More deliberate. Weighing a good deal more. And strangely troubling in its intensity.

I was with a group of people, none of whom I recognized. A family with a son, perhaps in his late teens or early twenties. I noticed the quality of light in the room: thick pea-soup yellow-green engulfing us all, holding us together as if to say: *You are responsible for one another.* I knew that the son's parents and everyone else of authority claimed the young man had committed a crime and must be punished. I heard myself, as if from beyond my body, arguing there'd been no crime. *The boy is innocent*, I said, *falsely accused.*

A slow-motion dance ensued. Multiple hands reaching to batter the young man. My hands moved out against them, grabbing to protect him from a moment I knew would result in false charges, certain conviction, decades of imprisonment.

I felt that I must shelter this youth, who didn't seem to notice me. He was Caucasian, thin, with ashy blond hair cut close to his head. He had a narrow face and cranium, as if an invisible vice had pressed it into elongated fear. His eyes—pale and glass-like and staring at a point beyond the picture plane—were empty of expression. He bore the scars of a society in which he'd never found a place to stand. I pitied but didn't want to touch him.

I stepped out of the dream for a moment, to ask myself why the young man was white. Most of the wrongly imprisoned youth in this country are black or brown. *Equal opportunity*, I mused, then succumbed to a force that felt stronger than gravity, pulling me back in.

The scene shifted and, without losing sight of the youth and his family, I was lying on my back upon a bed. Beside me lay Che Guevara. The revolutionary icon looked as he did in Mexico before boarding the *Granma* for Cuba and sailing off to help liberate the *first free territory of the Americas*. The doctor on his journey to immortality via a map he forged as he went.

We were both fully clothed, Che in the dark green military uniform that would characterize him throughout the rest of his life, me in a light copper-colored shift of glistening silk, high-necked and long-sleeved, clinging to my body. The me who observed the me on the bed could see that the fabric was torn in places, a loose thread here, a seam beginning to split there. We didn't speak as he began caressing me. His hands were gentle. They knew my secret places. I can still feel them as I write. The experience wasn't sexual but deeply sensual. I felt both relaxed and excited by his touch.

Then my youngest daughter, Ana, appeared. She began calling out to Che, perhaps trying to get his attention for some reason I ignored, perhaps attempting to get him to leave her mother alone. Her gestures were animated but I couldn't make out what she was saying. All I saw were her hands and lips moving, punctuated by wild motions set against a darkening sky. A storm hovered on the horizon: ominous clouds, bright darts of lightning. In dreams one can move effortlessly from indoors to out, the weather as fluid as fractals backlit by one too many suns.

I could tell that Ana was trying to convince Che of something. I strained to hear, all the while continuing to enjoy the man's hands playing across my body: breasts, belly, thighs. No genital contact. At last Ana's words sounded in my ears. She was saying goodbye to the hero of my youth. As she did so, she casually addressed him as *Trump*.

Of course, the mistaken identity bolted me from my pleasure. Was this a slip of the tongue or intentional. *Not Trump*, I cried. *Why did you call him Trump?* She denied she had done so, and I insisted, looking around for concurring expressions of others who might have overheard. The family with the son was in the picture once more, but no one corroborated what I was saying. I kept trying to convince Ana of her mistake. She kept denying she'd uttered the repugnant name.

And then I was emerging from sleep, that one-way ticket that erases the possibility of return, leaving my dream behind, although bits and pieces of it stuck to my skin like static electricity sticks to newly washed clothes.

There are dreams that follow me for days, nudging my consciousness with their broken shards of angst. There are nightmares that terrorize long after I'm fully awake. This dream was different. It's been more than a week now and it still sits on my shoulder, whispering in my ear, insisting it is no more nor less than itself.

Mocking. Self-satisfied. Daring me to enter its map and walk, restoring memory one burning fragment at a time.

Visitation

In conversation with Bob Arnold

Old poet friends keep walking out of letters, emerging from conversations, even appearing with one raised eyebrow from the pages of a book. On their way to visit, they may stumble on a broken curb or hit a rough patch of trail, broken earth, or concrete. I wait, hand extended, ready to catch them before they go down. I want to spend more time together, retrieve their memories, the bursts of light and bits of connective tissue that fit my own like the mislaid pieces of an elaborate jigsaw puzzle. A segment may look as if it doesn't interlock with the empty space that I carry on my back but look closer: a slight curve or indentation tells a different story.

I welcome Janine Pommy Vega, young and fearless as she crosses the Hudson from New Jersey and makes her way to New York's Lower East Side. She is sixteen years old and with a girlfriend whose name we never learn. They find the Beat poets they are looking for, naturally in the tenor of the times ending up in Peter Orlovsky's and Gregory Corso's beds. This is Janine's calling card, but the woman who will make her mark as a unique and brilliant poet understands that Peter and Allen Ginsberg inhabit another register, physically as well as in future tense. This was her entrance, nothing more. Later she finds her Fernando and they make a life together until he dies with a heroin needle in his arm. She has other lovers, but those relationships aren't the same. In his moving memoir,[1] Bob Arnold writes that those who saw Janine in the last six years of her life were watching a woman dying. It's hard to say when most people begin dying, except in retrospect. The clues may be there, but we aren't trained to notice.

Others who've recently come to visit: Roque Dalton, Juan Gelman, Robert Creeley, Julio Cortázar, Ann Quin, Allen Ginsberg, Denise Levertov, Carol Bergé, Paul Blackburn, Joel Oppenheimer, George Hitchcock, Janice Gould, Thomas Merton, Bladamir Zamora, Akilah Oliver, Bobby Louise Hawkins, Audre Lorde, June Jordan, Adrienne Rich, and Ernesto Cardenal. There is no order to their appearance. The more recent departures—Mel Buffington, Chely Lima—are beginning to visit but only briefly. I think they are still uncertain as to how long they may stay without risking being unable to return to wherever it is they currently reside. Discipline still calls.

Creative spirits who spent their lives making poems against the obstacles society erects. Maybe poets possess a seventh sense, a set of tricks we use to fool the statisticians, those who make the rules and hide the keys to the calendars, the moral cowards and literal record keepers. Walter and Lilian Lowenfels tumbled from a friend's letter today. Her paralysis had disappeared, and he no longer had to carry her up and down stairs, help her across uncertain thresholds. Still, they look like they did when they visited me in Mexico in 1964. Back then I showed Lilian something I'd written, and she admonished me for misspelling the word *mouths*: an unnecessary *e* before the *s*. I never really knew if it was my lack of formal education that made me such a bad speller or if I just didn't pay enough attention. Lilian's correction was firm but kind. She didn't dwell. And I never again misspelled that word. In time, I achieved a formal literary skill, perhaps by osmosis.

Now I remember the four of us struggling slowly up several flights of narrow stairs to visit another poetic couple, Agustí and Ana Bartra,

---

1. *Faraway Like the Deer's Eye, a Saga* (Vermont: Longhouse Publications, 2023).

Catalan victims of Spain's civil war exiled in Mexico. Sergio and I dragged Walter and Lilian behind, Walter struggling with Lilian's unwieldy weight. The brutal shock of McCarthyism had caused her to suffer a stroke and she moved with difficulty for the rest of her life. It was only a physical difficulty, though, her mind forever sharp.

Our breakfast with David Alfaro Siqueiros and his wife Angelica also swims to the surface now. Walter wanted the great muralist to do a series of original drawings for the book of his we would publish under *El Corno Emplumado's* imprint.[2] Siqueiros was delighted to comply. Recently Sergio regifted me with that breakfast bearing a story I'd forgotten. As we shared the typical *huevos rancheros* and black beans, Siqueiros gesticulated wildly, a bouffant tie he was wearing always threatening to graze the *molcajete* filled with hot sauce sitting in the center of the table. *Mira la corbata*, Angelica chided him again and again, *Watch your tie, David!* Until Siqueiros, annoyed by her frequent interruptions, loosened the broad ribbon around his neck and thrust it into the hot sauce as if to say *Basta ya, enough of that, already!*

Walter told me that the night before Lilian died, she raised her eyes and begged him not to forget to pay her monthly Communist Party dues. He made sure she was up to date with her support. Walter and I corresponded until his own death. He walked me back to poets who never got the message or simply defied the mandate the witch hunt imposed: that we shouldn't write about social issues, that politics had no place in poetry. He introduced me to the work of Sonia Sanchez, Clarence Major, Olga Cabral. I hadn't realized they were spurned by the academy. In Mexico, where I then made my home, poets wrote about everything.

Roque always appears in leprechaun mode, a disguise as different from his Salvadoran culture as is possible to imagine. Although disguise itself

2. *Land of Roseberries / Tierra de moras*, by Walter Lowenfels, Spanish translation by Sergio Mondragón and Margaret Randall, drawings by David Alfaro Siqueiros (Mexico City: El Corno Emplumado, 1965).

is pertinent to his history. He always has some new and astonishing tale to tell. We never talk about what's on my mind, only his. Will he be riding with the Dalton Gang of my own country's Wild West or trying to ground himself in dark resignation as he realizes his own comrades are about to end his life? When he leaves, I move about the room, gathering the shards of Vallejo he's scattered while here.

Once he found his missing granddaughter who had been adopted into an Argentinean military family when her mother was tortured to death by that same military, Juan could die in peace. The long search had taken its toll. A terminal illness had been eating away at him for months, perhaps years. While in this unholy North, poets of my generation were still being warned not to write about "politics," that catchall category decried off limits to the creative mind, Juan, unencumbered by such specious directives, wrote about nothing but. It appeared in his poems with the power of a Beethoven symphony. He created a language recognized by academy and hungry reader alike.

I always shudder when Carol appears moments before dawn. I'm in no mood for her drug-induced conniving, calculated promises, bedrock of conservative politics set to trip me up behind her seductive voice. I want to forget the abuse she heaped upon her young son when they visited us in Mexico City, how we couldn't even name that then but recoiled at what we simply saw as meanness. Years later, she ended up in Santa Fe, not far from me. And the push/pull continued: pleading smile one day, devious invitation another. Next time around I will ask if she remembers the memorial where friends and associates emphasized her difficult nature and I opted to speak only about her work: that edge of possibility.

Together, Akilah and I remember our first conversation. She sat in the room's only armchair, I on the edge of the bed in the motel adjacent to Naropa's campus of a Boulder summer. We were both visiting professors at that year's Summer Writing Program. She said she wanted to get to know me. I wanted to get to know her but would probably have been too shy had she not made the first move. We talked about her son, recently gone, and the trauma remaining in his wake. We talked about language, its power to convey and perhaps even heal such tragedy. She was excited about an upcoming study program in Switzerland, unaware she would be denied its delights. One thing about death: it radically alters our plans.

Denise, when she appears, is always impeccably dressed. A tidy English war nurse, the poet simmering beneath the surface. We may begin by reminiscing about her visit to us in 1960s Mexico City, but soon I am throwing questions at her, questions that still need answering for me. How did you evolve from your early homophobia, or did you? Did you always feel good about freeing a fellow poet's mind from its prison bars and releasing it to a nationwide readership? Have you kept up with the voices of our great women poets Do they speak to you?

Joel and I will always begin and end by talking about our son, no other conversation possible. There are no recriminations because I chose to have Gregory without telling him, selfishly ignoring his right to weigh in. Father and son found their way to each other much later, on their own, and I applauded their coming together. Joel and I can delight in the relationships all his sons have nurtured with one another, overriding those social conventions that establish sad categories such as *half-brother* or *stepson*. Even their various mothers experience a sense of family. The poetry is icing on the cake.

Janice remains silent during the first moments of our post-death visits. It's about her indigenous custom of keeping important emotions close to the breast. It's not that she doesn't have a lot to say: lesbian daughter of a Maidu mother and English father who transitioned in his seventies to become a woman named Barbara. Janice continues to surprise by revealing one more astonishing twist from her past, competence on another musical instrument, or a new level of skill in the practice of a martial art. Sometimes she still seems physically weakened by the sudden struggle of her dying, but her profound knowing floats to the surface then, opening doors.

Thomas Merton and I know we will always have something more to discuss about faith and social change. The eternal God dilemma. He will be patient with my goading, we agree on all terrestrial matters. George Hitchcock retains his looming figure even in death. Gentleness still drips from his fingertips. There is a mustiness in the air when he arrives, announcing some mysterious unknown quality. Yet I never ask him to explain. What wasn't clear in life cannot be explored in later visitation. Ann Quin still walks, walks, into a never-ending ocean of relief. Cortázar is gentle too, his oversized extremities fighting him every step of the way. His hands are shovels now. Moisture seeps from beneath Creeley's eye patch; it seems our infirmities don't let go, even in death.

Adrienne assures me she is no longer in pain, but there are no more poems; she's said it all. Bladamir, on the other hand, talks long and hard. I realize the Cuban country drawl and those silences he practiced when he lived were screens he placed between himself and society's judgment. Now he tells beautiful tales of lovers caressing one another in shadowy corners, ideas flying free, all that should have seen the elegant light of equality before rum took its final toll. Bobby Louise observes us all with a whimsical smile, perhaps writing the perfect story in her mind as she takes care to keep from tripping over the coils of long plastic tubing that feed her tired lungs.

Sometimes I think I always moved slowly and with erratic step, took a long time to catch up. Even with myself. Perhaps a product of my provincial upbringing. I sought out one after another concentric circle of creative people. Some of us thought we could change the world. Others knew the only change we could make was to language and ideas, broad palettes of our passions. When I was young, those artists of image and word took me to themselves in ways I simply accepted at the time. Already having achieved some measure of success, they nevertheless reached out to lift my incipient talent. Looking back, I marvel that they saw something in me I didn't yet see. At some point the coming and going became a single heartbeat. We all moved together. Now I am no longer the youngest among us but often the oldest. I try to imagine how I can be for those coming up what my mentors and friends were for me.

Empathy

ately I've been obsessed with a question about human development and almost every conversation I have, book or article I read, even what I choose to cook for dinner or how the weather announces itself when I part the blinds each morning, tickles this question in some unexpected way. Simply put: why and how did the earliest humans stray from the necessary self-involvement required to protect themselves against danger—bitter cold, extreme heat, hunger, pain, the threat of wild animals—and begin to factor into their natures a concern for others, what we define as generosity of spirit or empathy? In other words, when and how did humans become human? At a time when so many humans not only seem pointedly inhuman, neofascist politicians encourage them to be so, and anything resembling empathy is absent from public discourse, the question seems particularly relevant.

One might extend my question to animals, most of whom demonstrate caring feelings toward others of their species.[3] Some animals even display

---

3. In *Our Inner Ape* (Riverhead Books, 2005), Frans de Waal uses carefully documented data as well as anecdotal evidence to support the idea that animal behavior displays instinctual emotional empathy.

such feelings toward those of another species (the cat who adopted a litter of puppies; the lioness who cared for oryx calves; the giant tortoise who made friends with a baby hippo). We speak of these relationships as instinctual and (naively) ask if the nurturing animal is aware that it is caring for one that isn't of its kind. All animals act instinctively, and non-human mammals certainly have emotions. Without the ability to think like dog people or elephant people, we tend to observe animal behavior through our own androcentric lens, and this prevents us from understanding who they are.

So, I want to be clear: I don't believe humans are unique in possessing empathy. Every living being probably cares for others of their, and even other, species. Right now, however, my obsession is focused on humans and on our general inclination toward the humane. I credit both nature and nurture in our development. And I am curious about when and how human beings moved from primarily being concerned with our own survival to demonstrating compassion for others.

Again, to be clear, I am not speaking of selflessness or selfishness. It is not selfish to exercise the life force, perhaps our strongest instinct. Mothers are universally protective of our young, and there is ample evidence that this has been so throughout time. I am interested in the tendency to extend that instinct toward others and when and how it arose in our long history of evolution.

Sympathetic qualities vary from person to person, ranging all the way from those "bad seeds" who seem to have been born evil and thus possess none of them, to the most altruistic among us. In general, though, as Anne Frank is quoted as having said in her darkest days, "I still believe most people are good at heart."[4] In every culture, independent of

---

4. Anne Frank (1929–1945) was a young Jewish girl in occupied Holland who hid with her family in an attic and kept a diary of the experience that was found after the war and became one of the all-time most read books. The family was denounced and discovered shortly before the war's end, and Anne died from typhus at Bergen-Belsen concentration camp.

the formalistic attributes it may project, most people will share what they have if presented with someone in need. Someone who is in danger or hungry, cold, ill. The most dramatic situations often result in the most extraordinary gestures; for example, when non-Jews hid Jews during the Second World War, or in today's context of Russia's invasion of Ukraine in which families throughout Europe have welcomed Ukrainian refugees into already crowded homes. Such empathy may be as instinctual as it is virtuous, but it also responds to a learned philosophy that posits caring for others as a moral imperative.[5] Way back in the shadows of history, where did this practice of lending a helpful hand come from? What motivated it? And how did it develop? When we wonder, we wander. This is where I wander today.

COVID fore fronted the question of helping our neighbors, checking to see who among them might need attention, someone to go to the grocery store or help with other routine needs. Perhaps that two-year period, from which we have only recently emerged, brought this question to my mind. But it feels older, more primal. I imagine life millions of years ago (what historians, foolishly I believe, call pre-history) when our ancestors struggled to stay safe, keep warm, eat enough to survive, reproduce, and create. I imagine their daily battle for food and protection, repeated over and over from an age of reason to death. Necessities were crude and may often have eluded possibility. A powerful survival instinct must have consumed those early humans. Why and when and how did they make the time and hone the effort to spend a portion of their energy on others?

Perhaps some followed an instinct to be generous and others witnessed their actions, saw something they liked, and mimicked them. Because humankind was at the threshold of discovery, our ancestors didn't yet have

---

5. When Gay Block and Malka Drucker interviewed more than 100 non-Jews, in 11 countries, who at great personal risk hid Jews from the Nazis, almost all of them said they did so because it was "the right thing to do." They simply hadn't considered doing otherwise. Quoted in *Rescuers: Portraits of Moral Courage in the Holocaust*, 1992, reissued by Radius Books in 2020.

the variety of inventions we have today, neither those which are genuinely helpful nor those which advertise as such but dampen or hinder our natural abilities. They had no help lines, vitamin supplements, antidepressants, special education, or experts in a variety of psychological and emotional areas. No substance abuse programs or anger management classes. Consulting was a ruse that would not exist for hundreds of generations. We cannot know for sure, but it seems unlikely that the people I am thinking of had courses in citizenship or other recipes for comportment. Mentorship was probably an early road to this sort of practice, perhaps the earliest. As humans developed and progressed, they must have learned from observing their elders.

I go to ancient texts—Gilgamesh, Homer, the Old Testament Psalms, Nezahualcóyotl. I read contemporary biologists and social scientists such as De Waal and Bateson. I find ideas that send me in one direction or another, but nothing that focuses precisely on my question. And clues are often double-edged or contradictory. De Waal reminds us that "biology is usually called upon to justify a society based on selfish principles, but we should never forget that it has also produced the glue that holds communities together."[6]

We tend to believe life was simpler in ancient times, that our ancestors weren't plagued by classism, racism, gender discrimination or homophobia. Although belief in the supernatural was a fallback position for early humans, I can't imagine that organized religion promoted the hierarchies, prejudices, and injustices it does today. Neither do we imagine our ancient forebears screaming at one another over political differences that are increasingly polarizing and with less and less possibility of acknowledging a common ground. But was this really the case, or did these positions simply evidence themselves differently from how they do now?

Was it their need for companionship that sparked generosity of spirit? Did our ancestors realize that if they didn't dedicate a certain amount of

---

6. *The Age of Empathy* by Frans De Waal, p. x.

effort to bringing others—family members, those in their communities or tribes—along, they would pay the price of loneliness? The death of those around them must have been a terrible thing for those people. Death continues to be a terrible thing, perhaps the most terrible, but now we at least understand its inevitability. In the almost unknown world of those early people, confusion must have accompanied the anguish of loss. A good friend who recently lost her partner of thirty years, describes the months leading up to his death as being filled with "a foreboding, a constant edge of fear." And although as prepared as she could be, when it happened, she was devastated. As I grieved for my friend, I also tried to imagine such a situation hundreds of thousands of years ago, among people for whom what they themselves experienced was their only guide.

Competition produces a failure of empathy and greed is the result. In this sense, the industrial revolution undoubtedly had a great deal to do with a massive departure from the principle of caring. In the early years of the Cuban revolution, I witnessed the effort to replace competition with emulation; a group decided on a common goal and the members of that group helped one another to achieve it. This looked promising in neighborhoods, classrooms, the workplace, and other venues. Eventually, though, worldwide capitalist hegemony caused the tiny island nation to stray from some of its more altruistic goals. The pressure to compete was simply too great.

In today's world we have several widespread examples of the absence of empathy. The ease with which we initiate and sustain war is the greatest. Another is the angry shooter who attacks a school, social club, or theater. Yet another is the prevalence of bullying among young people, a situation that in recent years has reached pandemic proportions. Today's society has spawned hatred as a weapon—against people of color, gay and trans people, women. And there are the men who mistreat or exploit women: fathers their daughters, husbands their wives, and in general the males of our species conditioned to assume a sense of entitlement with all those they consider subservient. Unimaginable for most of us and yet tragically common are mothers who refuse to protect their daughters from fathers who sexually abuse them. Motherlove is a deep and millennial instinct, yet many mothers take their husband's side against their daughters, either because they choose not to believe them, out of economic dependence, or simple apathy. This is a social phenomenon that defies our ability to empathize.[7]

As with any impulse, when I think about solidarity, I also consider those who take it to an extreme. We all know people who bend over backwards to do for others, often things those others haven't asked for and don't want. The "helpers" in this case suffer from a condition in which they see their own worth reflected in such actions. I doubt that ancient humans suffered from such personality disorders. They must have had their hands full simply caring for themselves and those who really needed their help.

I mention these contemporary variations on the subject of human empathy to illustrate its complexity in societies in which a variety of philosophical considerations impact our emotional responses. The question that compels me reaches back to a remote past before such considerations took their toll. Like some obstinate feedback loop, I inevitably seem to end up with examples of exceptions to empathy rather than its human origins.

When we sacrifice even a small portion of our own wellbeing to help or care for someone else, it is a choice. When did our ancestors become aware they had such choices, decide to make them, and why? It is all conjecture, of course. No matter how much fresh information social anthropologists produce from examining the sites where people lived, and implements, bones and biomatter, I will never know.

---

7. Although many of us have private stories of mothers who have abandoned their daughters to male sexual abuse, there is a public story that is iconic. In 1998 Zoilamérica Ortega spoke publicly about her stepfather having raped her almost daily for 19 years, beginning at age 11. Ortega is the president of Nicaragua. His wife and vice-president, Rosario Murillo, opted to defend her husband and abandon her daughter. Despite irrefutable evidence of their crime, there are many who refuse to question the Ortega/Murillo regime.

My obsession with when and how our earliest ancestors first began thinking of their contemporaries as well as themselves leads to further questions. For example, when did we begin to think in abstractions rather than only in terms of the practical here and now? What role does art play in linking mind to desire? The answers to these questions seem to be hiding just out of reach. As if I might turn a corner and find them waiting in unexplored memory.

Figure 3

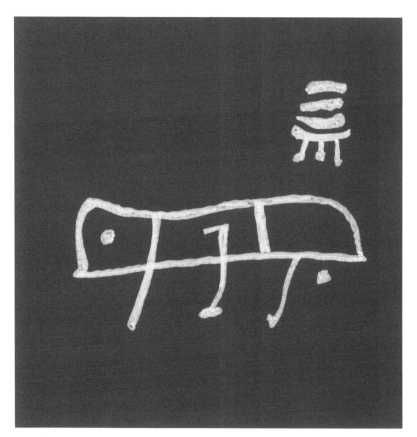

Figure 4

Cruel Sex

wonder if humans are the only female animals who accept or even desire cruelty in their sexual encounters. Particularly women. Not all women, of course, but a significant number, at least in the cultures I've inhabited, prefer to be mistreated than loyally cherished and gently loved. The abuse is not always what we would call brutal: living in constant danger of physical beatings or worse, although our societies endure their share of serious domestic threat and follow-through. As we've learned more about this patriarchal phenomenon, we've created hotlines, shelters, and even police units specially trained to deal with victims. We've begun to hold some of the offenders accountable. We've improved our laws, although they're still not what we need.

But I'm straying from my subject. I'm not talking about gross physical or psychological abuse here, but something less violent and perhaps more prevalent: the attraction many women feel for a partner who can be psychologically abusive, aloof, selfish, mean, or disdainful. A significant other or occasional lover who excites her by showing her who's boss. This quality acts as a sexual draw for many women. I'm not talking about bondage, sadomasochism, or other examples of extreme sexual behavior in which all involved agree on certain conditions and rules. And I'm not now focusing on the male proclivity for abuse, but on the fact that some females seek it out.

What I'm talking about are sexual encounters in which the man is demanding but dismissive, and the woman knows she is there for his pleasure, a momentary plaything subjected to his timetable, convenience, and desire.

The allure some women feel for sexual bullying and even danger is one of patriarchy's least discussed footprints. Chemistry plays a part in what we call *falling in love*, but healthy long-term relationships are based on trust, compassion, caring, mutual support, and stability. We women, though, are conditioned from before we are born to want *strong*, and it can be a small step from *strong* to *too strong*. As in *it's just his nature*. Or *he gets carried away*. Or *it's not his fault; he doesn't know his own strength*. Or *I know there's no future in it, but I can't help myself*. Rather than demand in their partners the respect they should be demanding from themselves, such women will excuse the violent partner's ugly behavior. Or more to my point, seek it out.

I am not among these women. Twice in my life, a sexual partner started slapping me around as we were making love. I was shocked to the point of comedown and repulsion. In both cases, I extricated myself from the offender's embrace, fled the scene, and refused to reengage.

My father loved my mother from the moment he saw her, and never stopped loving her until his death 62 years later. My mother said she married him on the rebound, believing he would be a good provider, husband, and father; although I suspect she came to care for him in her own way. He was gentle and sweet, forgave her many transgressions, once left her for a couple of months but came back convinced theirs was the relationship he wanted. She had begged him to return, promising she would *never be bad again*. Meaning she would stop having frequent flings with impervious lovers who treated her dismissively but lured her into their seductive nets of entitlement. My parents' relationship quickly went back to the pattern she needed and he endured.

What I witnessed growing up was typical serial infidelity on the one hand, made more confusing because, on the other, it was the woman who transgressed rather than the man. Early on I blamed her and sympathized with him. It took me years to understand that she was acting out of a damage she couldn't name, much less address. Witnessing both my parent's pain over a long period of time is one of the things that got me thinking about this topic.

Toward the end of my mother's life, we talked about her marriage. Dad had been gone for a decade. She confessed that none of her many affairs had satisfied her in any real way. I asked her why she kept having them, and she said *I wanted to be loved.* The love she was looking for had to be illicit and include that component of one-sided power. Dad's consistent considerate loving just didn't do it for her.

At this point I might explore Mother's childhood, which offers plenty of clues as to why she only felt physical attraction for men who used and abused her. Her father, my grandfather, sexually molested me when I was an infant and there's ample evidence that he did the same to her. I prefer to look at the phenomenon in more general terms. I'm not an expert in animal behavior, but I suspect that other animals—mammals, amphibians, reptiles, fish, birds, and insects—observe patterns that satisfy their needs for comfort, survival, and reproduction. And that those patterns rely on pleasure as an element of enticement. We often make the mistake of judging other species through the human lens. It is entirely possible that these creatures experience their own versions of loyalty, jealousy, solidarity, or mean-spiritedness. But I cannot imagine the females of those species seeking exploitative encounters for purely emotional reasons.

Can patriarchal dominance alone account for so many women courting those who will treat them badly? Are women raised to think so little of ourselves that many of us believe we deserve, even need, mistreatment at the hands of a lover? Does seeking abuse provide a panacea for some sense of inadequacy we cannot name? Is emotional pain an inherited or natural element in sexual satisfaction for some women? Perhaps today's routine overstimulation of the senses creates a need for the sort of touch—physical or emotional—that goes beyond what most of us would find acceptable. None of these explanations seem the whole answer to me.

I believe that if we were encouraged to explore our pasts, name those who have abused us, and reclaim our power (or claim it for the first time), we would hide fewer secrets around our diverse sexualities and would be able to talk more openly about what each of us needs and wants without the social tabus that keep us silent or barely whispering among ourselves. If we could discuss sex without fear of social stigma, religious dogma, or the lie that men need while women must fulfil that need, I think abuse might lose its appeal.

No dark regions would remain in which any form of cruelty is experienced as thrilling.

Serial Marriage

My parents' marriage spanned 62 years, from their two different memories regarding the year they got together until my father's death—one claimed it was 1932, the other 1933. A very brief parenthesis took place during my teenage years when Dad, frustrated by Mother's succession of affairs, left for a few weeks. She begged him to return, promising to *be good*. And he did return, perhaps convinced that putting up with her infidelities was preferrable to living without her. There was no physical violence in my childhood home, but it was characterized by constant frustration and resulting outbursts of tension.

I was married or lived for considerable lengths of time successively with six men and one woman before Barbara, my wife of 37 years, and I found one another. Many would consider this an unusually extensive list of long-term partners. Until just a few years ago, I was shamed by my proclivity to leave one when I felt that I was suffocating, or it became clear to me that the situation was no longer tenable. My behavior was contrary to the unwritten code of ethics women of my class and culture were expected to uphold. One of the accusatory questions I remember the government lawyer asking me during my 1986 immigration hearing was: "Is it true,

Ms. Randall, that your children have three different fathers?" I understood that the question was meant to diminish me.

I was annoyed by such a denigration of how I've lived my life. A fierce inner conviction kept me from doubting the wisdom of getting out of a relationship that limited me or, in some cases, did me harm. What reason could I possibly have for staying? Many miserable couples stick it out for their children, believing nothing will hurt them more than a broken home. My own parents gave this as one of the reasons they stayed together. I have always thought that children of divorce are healthier and happier than they would be if forced to remain with a model of constant marital dissatisfaction, or worse.

Looking back, I realize that I married the first time because I thought it was the only way a young woman of my generation could escape her parental home. Although I couldn't see it at first, my husband was mentally ill and psychologically abusive. Four years later I divorced him and breathed a long sigh of relief. I had my first child with a later lover, *out of wedlock* as the condition was described at the time. I took my infant son to Mexico, where I met and married a poet with whom I lived for eight years, and we had two daughters. We shared an intense creative life but the day he joined a religious cult that proclaimed women couldn't attain nirvana I knew the marriage was over.

My next relationship was with a US American poet whose culture was more attuned to mine. With him too I had a child, my youngest daughter. My time with her father bridged some of the more dramatic events of my life: the political repression I suffered in Mexico, the resultant need to send our four young children to Cuba, and my underground journey to join them there. But after another eight years—I came to fear that would be as long as I would ever be able to live with a spouse—that relationship ended as well.

A Colombian poet was my last major love interest in Latin America before returning to the United States. Home once more, after almost a quarter century's absence, I lived briefly with another North American poet with whom I'd previously enjoyed a platonic friendship. We married, something I'm sure many believed I did to help secure residency and eventually get my US citizenship back. But that wasn't the case. I thought I was in love with the man. In retrospect, I can see that the feeling reflected a way of easing a painful transition. Our marriage lasted a year.

It was then, at age fifty, that I realized I loved women. Why so late in life? Perhaps because the sort of political involvement I'd engaged in south of the border kept me from examining personal desire. Perhaps because the countries where I'd lived didn't yet have embracing lesbian communities, safe spaces in which to explore my intimate need. Although I was as surprised as anyone by the change, I'd never been one to avoid following my instinct. I had an almost year-long relationship with a woman with whom I was absolutely unsuited before I met Barbara. She and I have been together for the past 37 years. We recognized one another immediately and moved in with one another days after our first date. In 2013, when marriage equality became federal law, we made the relationship legal.

Each time I've entered a serious relationship I've done so believing myself in love and hoping the union would last. What makes my partnership with Barbara different? It works for many reasons, among them the fact that we are both artists who love one another's work and have never known a moment of competition or jealousy. Each is inspired by the other's mind and continues to be excited by the other's body even as advancing age changes its contour and texture. Tenderness is a valued currency. Our social classes and cultures of origin couldn't have been more different, yet we see the world in the same way. Practically, we don't keep track of who does what in our home—no lists tacked to the refrigerator door. Each of us just notices what needs to be done and takes pleasure in doing more than her "part." We value loyalty and kindness, with a necessary quota of silliness. But none of this truly explains what we have and, as I grasp for explanation, it all sounds a bit cliched. Perhaps much of our happiness comes down to the fact that we are simply older and have learned what it means for two people to live together: the challenges and joy. Or maybe it's just great good luck, strengthened by rock solid commitment.

This narrative of serial marriages and marriage-like relationships speaks to the fact that, despite society's rigid codes I wasn't afraid to try, fail, and try again until I got it right: a union in which to grow and help another do the same. Yet in my class and culture, my journey reads like that of the proverbial *loose woman*, certainly one who broke with convention at every turn. In my generation, while unmarried men were called *bachelors*, unmarried women bore the stigma of *spinster* or *old maid*. Similarly, no one was concerned when men moved from one relationship to another. When women did the same, they were seen as morally questionable. I'm fortunate that I've never felt overly affected by that social double standard.

I refuse to shoulder the responsibility for what I consider to be society's problem. The hypocrisy inherent in so many patriarchal values affects men as well as women, but women immeasurably more. I say we place the blame where it belongs and not allow it to keep us from finding what works for us: in intimate relationships, belief systems, creative pursuits, chosen careers, parenting decisions, and where we wish to live.

I witnessed my parents, two good people, exhaust themselves through a decades-long marriage that shouldn't have been. They were of a generation that believed that vows were forever and putting a good face on a bad situation was what mattered. They disparaged psychotherapy or other practices which might have helped them achieve happier lives. When my brother told our father he was leaving his first wife, Dad responded: "You can't do that. Your mother and I haven't been happy, but you don't see me leaving, do you?" I have often wondered what life might have been like for my parents if they'd had the courage to follow their dreams. Witnessing their misery taught me there had to be something better. Barbara and I inhabit a joy beyond my capacity for description.

I've titled this piece "Serial Marriage." I'm not sure the name fits but can't think of a better one. *Serial monogamy* describes the practice of entering and leaving relationships as desire dictates, while remaining faithful in each as long as it lasts. *Serial marriage* implies a similar route sanctioned by the State. I entered each of my long-term relationships believing they were forever. When they went bad, I tried to salvage the situation. When that wasn't possible, I didn't hesitate to leave. I always hoped I had learned something that would make the next partnership, if there was one, more successful.

Even when harmful, we tend to replicate behaviors we experience in our youth. If we grow up in dysfunctional homes, we swear we'll act differently from our parents. And when a relationship doesn't work for us, we believe we will make a better choice the next time around. But good intentions aren't always enough. We may exit a bad union and enter one that seems to be its opposite in every way, only to learn too late that we are facing the same problems in another disguise. Too often patterns have been established that are difficult to break. Sometimes we need to exhaust one experience after another before we get it right.

It excites me to see that young people today are far less constrained by hypocritical social mores. To an important extent they are rejecting unhealthy behaviors, discarding outmoded customs, and embodying more egalitarian ways of relating to one another. Many are refusing the either/or of binary thinking and exploring new, more authentic ways of being. Today, although the road is filled with fear and hatred, there is a future for trans people and others who don't fit into the old social molds. Feminism has cracked the patriarchy open, even as we still have a long journey ahead.

Counting

count. I don't mean that I am worth something but that I verbalize numbers: one, two, three, etc. It is an activity like any other, occupying its
own time and space on any given day. I've always counted, only realized
rather late in adolescence that it wasn't on the list of approved activities. I
kept on counting then, but to myself.

I count the number of steps between landings on a flight of stairs, the
number of crows sitting on a telephone wire, the number of cars that go by
as I wait in ours for my wife to emerge from the post office. I count the number of stamps affixed to the package she carries, the audible seconds on a
clock, my silent breaths before you start speaking again, the beats in any
musical rhythm, the waxen leaves on the succulent sitting in its clay pot.

I count on my fingers or silently to myself. I imagine I will be required
to reveal the sum of my counting. It may be an emergency and I alone will
possess the answer. And so, I memorize numbers of steps, crows, seconds,
breaths.

My counting isn't simply an enumeration of crows or cars or stamps
or leaves. It means something. It can be a foreboding or a test. If I get to
one hundred before anyone speaks, it means you won't stop loving me. The
number of cars that pass may equate with the number of years of life I have

left. In entrusting my burning desire for old age to such chance, I know what a risk I am taking. Therein lies the challenge.

When I tell you something I know you don't want to hear, I count during the silence that precedes your response. You are thinking, feeling, considering what to say. I am counting. I know our love will survive. The counting is a bridge.

I used to tap a doorframe three times before entering a room. Once to my right, then twice to my left. I remember Mother telling me that a great grandmother I barely recall did the same. The story was conveyed as evidence that she was mentally ill. No one in their right mind would do such a thing. When I considered that, I stopped. This was important in my practice of counting: knowing I wasn't really compelled but could stop at any time. I counted but was in control.

But you know what? Counting is satisfying. Like doing a crossword puzzle or humming a tune, it is a harmless activity that passes the time and can keep you calm but alert, journeying along a pleasurable path. With all the violence and ugliness in the world, you wouldn't think anyone would object to a person counting to herself. Less harmful than bullying. Less boring than listening to advice about how not to put yourself in danger of being raped or robbed. If I'm raped or robbed, believe me, it won't be because I put myself in danger. I'll blame the perpetrator.

It was a night like any other. We'd been at the bar for hours, talking about art, sharing questions and stories. Just as on other nights, the man I'll call Bill and I walked out through balmy New York streets to my fourth-floor walkup. I understood that we would lie together on the mattress that almost filled my tiny bedroom floor. We barely spoke. I counted to myself as I undressed, as I watched him undress. I counted my breaths when we'd finished having sex and until he asked if I had anything to drink or said he'd better be going.

I counted as the intervals between labor pains came more rapidly, as those discrete pains became a single unbroken burst of agony and energy, as I felt the warm wet rush of the child's body emerge from mine, as the memory of that pain disappeared and only my baby's life remained. I repeated this counting, in English and then in Spanish, four times forever. I continue to count as my children give birth to children of their own and as their children have children.

I count the number of breaths I take in and expel when I reach the final rung of the 70-foot ladder and before being able to fully absorb the marvel that is Kiet Seel, even hundreds of years after its last inhabitant departed. I am standing at the high entrance to the ruin, on the stone ledge that runs along its face. Below the delta, once lush with squash and beans but now sandy and barren in the late afternoon sun, stretches out before me. I have hiked nine miles, stashed water bottles behind rocks, crossed and recrossed a stream with pockets of quicksand I'd been instructed to avoid by concentrating my mind and angling my feet. Sweat has turned dust to mud on my skin. I am breathing hard. The counting is arrival.

As the men with guns decide whether to shoot, I count to myself. I pay attention to trying to separate the digits by an equal number of seconds. This enables me to look them in the eyes without turning away. My counting provides a mirror in which they see what they are about to do. They lower their weapons. I keep on counting.

I wonder if I will have time to count as I am dying. I suspect it would ease the experience.

Anniversaries

Over a lifetime they accumulate but some sound louder in my ears than others.

The first atomic bombs, launched against the civilian populations of Hiroshima and Nagasaki on August 6 and 9, 1945. The executions of Ethel and Julius Rosenberg on June 19, 1953. Events I was too young to fully understand when they were perpetrated, but that have since taken up residence on my calendar of rage.

July 26, 1953: the day that launched the Cuban revolution. I had no idea at the time what an important place that revolution would have in my future. Twenty years after Cuba's victory, on July 19, 1979, the Sandinistas rescued Nicaragua from a dictatorial dynasty. We called it *the second free territory of the Americas.* I was older by then, and deeply involved in that struggle. I lived to participate in remaking that Central American country's society, one of the great moments of my life. I also lived long enough to witness its destruction, first from US intervention and counterrevolutionary maneuvering, and finally when some of the original Sandinistas' courage and conviction turned to arrogance and dictatorial control. Anniversaries are important but their meaning can be distorted by how faithful we are to their original premises.

Che Guevara's death on October 8, 1967, is an anniversary observed in almost every corner of the world where rebel spirits cling to hope in our ongoing need for change. I was living in Mexico City when the revolutionary was captured and executed on orders from the US Central Intelligence Agency (CIA). I continue to be able to feel the breath fleeing my lungs, replaced by a pain I cannot name. That night, with hundreds of others, I took to the streets, writing my rage on public walls.

For me, the date that hits hardest each time it comes around is October 2, 1968. On that day in Mexico City, government and paramilitary forces attacked a massive peaceful demonstration of students and others advocating for justice. At a place called the Plaza of Three Cultures—because high-rise apartment buildings were built over the remains of a colonial church which itself stands over pre-Colombian ruins—a flutter of white handkerchiefs signaled to tanks and helicopters. Death rained down on a crowd that had nowhere to flee but into the buildings. Bodies piled up in stairwells. Blood soaked the paving stones from ancient and modern times. Officialdom admitted to 26 dead; it is believed the number was closer to 1,000.

That was the day I learned what a government, when it feels threatened, is willing to do to its own people. I relive that knowledge every year.

April 25, 1975, is another date with special meaning to me, but it brings its yearly quota of celebration rather than despair. Like so many of my generation, I protested the US American war in Vietnam in every way I could. And in its final year, in the fall of 1974, I had the privilege of visiting that courageous country, traveling its devastated length, and interviewing women for a small book.[8] Just south of the 17th Parallel, in the liberated zone called Quang Tri, a group of wives and sisters patiently explained that the war would be over soon. *Your military is already defeated*, one woman

---

8. *Spirit of the People: Vietnamese Women Two Years from the Geneva Accords* (Vancouver: New Star Books, 1975 and *El espíritu de un pueblo* (Mexico City: Siglo XXI Editores, SA, 1975).

said through our interpreter, and smiled. Her smile held compassion as well as the conviction of victory. I remembered her words six months later as I watched televised scenes of the Vietnamese reclaiming their precious land.

September 11, 2001, is a date that almost everyone in the United States and many around the world acknowledge as a tragedy. On each anniversary I think of the terror the victims experienced and the families they left behind. And I also remember another September 11, the one in 1973, when forces of evil overthrew Chile's democratically elected Popular Unity government and Salvador Allende was forced to take his own life after promising that *one day the great avenues will open again, and the people will walk through.* Chileans eventually processed their years of dictatorship and, as I write, have elected another progressive government. The attack on US soil has never been adequately analyzed, though, and has been used to manipulate emotions from justifications for war to a skewed definition of patriotism that, far from redeeming us, has made us less safe.

There are many other anniversaries. Too many to enumerate here. Some I see coming each year and anguish or joy builds up in me, to be released on the day itself. Others have gotten lost in the folds of memory, and I think of them only in retrospect, wondering at how time has managed to erase them from my consciousness.

And then there are the intimate anniversaries marking family events. My son Gregory's birth on October 14, 1960. My daughter Sarah's on April 4, 1963, Ximena's on June 17, 1964, and Ana's on March 13, 1969. Sometimes, to my shame, I forget a grandchild or great grandchild's special day; our family has so many members now and age riddles my mind with failures of recall. My wife Barbara and I celebrate our anniversary on the Friday following Thanksgiving each year. We can no longer remember the day of the month and so refer to it as a *moveable feast.* My own birthday on December 6 continues to mean something every time it reappears; 87 years seems an accomplishment although I know it is only a marker.

Anniversaries are like mirrors. They reflect events both grim and joyous, what they mean to us, and most importantly what we make of them.

Hair

I n many cultures hair represents personal power. There's the Bible's Sampson, as one example. US Indigenous people who were sent to 20th century government boarding schools remember having their hair forcibly cut. The affront was in tandem with not allowing the students to speak their languages, practice their religions, dress as they had, or engage in other familiar cultural practices. Survivors often say that letting their hair grow long again brought back a stolen strength.

There's the hair on our heads and that which grows on other parts of our bodies: legs, underarms, genitalia, and inside elderly male ears. Fuzz on upper lips and chins is eagerly awaited by young white men while, at least in our culture, it often shames aging women. Indians and Asians typically have less body hair than Caucasians. A healthy underarm bush is considered sexy in France, a Brazilian wax job equally enticing in today's definition of glamour.

Hair means different things to different people. In outlawed polyga-mous Mormon families, the women are required not only to refrain from cutting their hair but to arrange it in prescribed ways that model submis-sion to fathers, brothers, husbands. Most fundamentalist religious sects hold similar attitudes about female hair. Contrary to the Indian belief that long hair means power; these women must submit to a custom that reflects a culture that keeps them powerless.

Hair is important to other religions in other ways: for Rastafarians uncut dreads hold a special meaning. The military, which is its own kind of religion, has its hair rule for men: the crew-cut that erases individuality. Sports like football, baseball and basketball encourage the same cut, prompting rebels such as Dennis Rodman to make alternative statements. Skinheads shave their heads as a sign of their racist stance. No wonder hippies and subsequent generations of rebellious youth sport long hair as a mark of nonconformity.

In many parts of the world, long hair for women and girls speaks male control. Men like to see their women with voluptuous tresses and the women, conditioned to please those men, comply. This is behind my wife Barbara's decision to shave her head. She was raised in a fundamentalist family and her long blonde locks were just one of the rules to which she was forced to submit. When she finally escaped her family's control, she got rid of her hair. But for years, she would explain that she was going to try to grow it out—you could sense how deeply she had been conditioned to feel ashamed of defying the convention. I would tell her to stop worrying, to go ahead and do what felt right, that which supported the self she needed. It took her a long time to stop experiencing the shame that had been beaten into her as a child.

Barbara has a beautifully shaped head. It looks good without hair. As she has been able to live more and more in her comfort zone, she has become radiant. But it's been a struggle. Sometimes people assume she's gone through chemotherapy or ask if she's a Buddhist nun. Few understand that a woman would shave her head for no "apparent" reason. Occasionally, upon hearing her explanation, another woman will say: "I wish I had the courage to do that." They don't mean it, not really.

I used to have long thick hair that was naturally wavy and didn't need more than washing and brushing. I loved my hair. Like Barbara's shaved head, my *crowning glory* made me feel complete: the way I wanted to look.

Clearly there was some social conditioning there, but my choice felt authentic to me. As I grew older, my hair went white and thin, revealing large patches of pink scalp. It was no longer my pride. I vividly remember the day I decided that my only option was to cut it short. It was like suddenly assuming a new identity, something that took a while to get used to. I drew a deep breath and plunged. But in my dreams, I still see myself with a full head of hair.

In our white-dominated society, African American hair has its particularities. It's only been in my lifetime that many Black women in the United States stopped torturing their hair with hot irons, straightening it into the stereotypical image of beauty seen through the Anglo-Saxon eye. I remember a great television skit in which Whoopi Goldberg put a white shirt on her head and tossed it back, referring to the shirt as *my beautiful long blond hair.*

Black pride, exemplified by Angela Davis and others, opened the door to afros, cornrows, Bantu knots, and similar brilliant sculptural fashions. But old shame dies hard. When I lived in Cuba, I picked my youngest daughter up at daycare one afternoon and was shocked to hear the teacher telling her charges to line up: *Those with good hair over here; those with bad hair over here.* She had a pick in one hand, a conventional comb in the other, and was about to prepare the children to go home for the day. That teacher was oblivious to the self-images and inhibitions she was passing on and, when I challenged her, told me I just wasn't familiar with how the islanders think about hair. *The words good and bad don't mean anything,* she argued. Slowly, Cuba's admiration for Angela encouraged many afro-Cuban women to rebel and reclaim their natural hair styles.

Today, Black men too may spend hours at a specialized barber shop, acquiring whatever intricate designs they want to adorn their heads. Young people of all races and cultures may dye their hair red or green or pink. Do's that take as long to create as ice sculptures reflect the unique personalities of those who wear them. And a shaved head, as well as the wildest fashion, may simply reflect a desire for freedom.

The Hug

won't say it was a silver lining, not in the usual meaning of the term. There was so much sickness and death. It would be disrespectful to speak of silver linings in such a time, not any we could discern. Better just to say I was relieved: hugging people you barely knew was no longer expected as it was before the pandemic.

I'm sure our culture didn't always encourage hugging as it does today. I must imagine there was a time when hugging or any sort of physical touch, was reserved for those you knew well: partner, parents, siblings, children and grandchildren, close colleagues, lifelong friends. It meant something special and wasn't to be dispensed gratuitously or reduced to a meaningless gesture by overuse. Different cultures observe different customs as well. For example, the kiss on both cheeks and its three-kiss version aren't common in the United States.

At some point in my adolescence the protocol around hugging changed. Could it have had something to do with the politics of the era? The 1950s overflowed with reserve. Our fear was well-founded. Perhaps we were reacting against Senator McCarthy's accusatory questions, Roy Cohn's refusal to come out of the closet even as he persecuted others for being gay. Part of our response may have included an overabundance of touch.

Rather than extend a hand or simply acknowledge another's presence verbally, it was more and more expected that you would grab them bodily. Or they you. Often without warning. The expected hug. You are introduced to someone and before you can draw back, they are upon you, clutching, patting your shoulder or back (or thigh?), depositing a kiss on your cheek. No invitation needed. That closeness. That heat. That scent. That weight.

In the context of today's cultural sensitivity, it is possible that the other person will stop briefly and ask: *Do you hug?* or just *May I?* But this only creates a few-second delay. The assault is upon you. Before you can accept or decline, you are trapped.

The discourse has changed, not the act.

The shift happened during COVID. Thus, the silver lining or relief I mentioned before. No longer must I allow strange arms to encircle me, strange breath to flood my nostrils, sudden unwanted touch on any part of my body. Gender had its impact as well. #MeToo promised consequences and for a brief time men feared them. Then backlash complicated cause and effect.

Now, because of the pandemic, it's acceptable to reject the hug without having to explain that I prefer close physical contact to be reserved for love, deep friendship, the intimacy that comes with a profound knowledge and appreciation of another human being. I can even lead with *I'm not hugging yet* and the incorrigible huggers will back off, smile, say of course they understand. People assume you're afraid of infection. If it weren't for the virus, you'd be kissing them on the lips.

I have a recurring dream. I am at a women's weekend workshop in the 1980s, somewhere in Rhode Island. This really happened. The workshop leader was an ex Dominican nun with a beautiful singing voice. We sat in a circle on the floor. The ex-nun wore a beatific smile. She instructed each woman to turn, face the woman to her right—we called all women sisters back then—and massage her shoulders. I refused, fled the room, carrying with me memories of myself in third grade when I fled my school playground after a bully music teacher tried to force me to sing a solo scale in front of my classmates. Dream and memory converge in my clenched fists.

It feels like we're in this new era for the long haul. Either COVID is here to stay, or we'll face further viruses. We'll accept a bad flu as inevitable once or twice a year.

People may stop wearing masks, no longer observe social distancing or wash their hands even before removing their coats when they get home. Will hugging creep back into our social interaction? Will my avoidance once more elicit that silent show of disapproval?

Will my excuse die an awkward death, or will I walk free?

Friends

The cyberworld has rearranged our identities and relationships in ways we couldn't have imagined just a few decades back. It's not only the vast access to information and the immediacy of the message. How we are presented and how we present ourselves have also changed. Some people are seduced into revealing things they wouldn't have put out there back when privacy still mattered. Some clearly believe every life event, from what they ate for breakfast to their favorite color is interesting. And the world responds. People have lost jobs or not been hired because of their social media profiles.

This ability to reveal oneself and so overtly interact with the world may be a panacea for loneliness. But it cannot be a healthy one.

Posts I read as utterly boring may receive hundreds or even thousands of *likes*. You can *like* or *love* a post; the first response is signaled by a thumbs-up icon in a blue circle, the second by a red heart. You can praise or insult. In today's shorthand culture, readers often prefer an emoticon—among them, those little yellow faces sporting a smile, a frown, a wink, even tears—to words they compose themselves. This is one of the things that troubles me; I fear they stand in for one's own thought process, self-expression, and creativity. Sometimes the person commenting feels compelled to outdo the original post with a bigger and more lavish animated message. Some of these are accompanied by sound. It won't be long before Harry Potter's motion-filled newspaper images are our everyday fare.

I'm particularly interested in that category called *friends*. People can request that you *friend* them, and you can do the same. When I entered the Facebook world, I accepted friend requests from anyone who asked, unless I actively disapproved of or disliked the person. Before I knew it, I had just short of 5,000. That's when I discovered that 5,000 is the limit unless you are a known personality. Oprah Winfrey, say, or a famous sports figure. They can have unlimited Facebook friends. I don't know if their fame alone gives them that prerogative or if they pay for the privilege. When I realized I would soon reach my limit, I began ignoring friendship requests, saving my final few in case a real friend asked.

Because I still believe in real friendships. In fact, they are the only ones that really count for me, and I treasure each. My almost 5,000 Facebook friendships exist in some cyberworld, but when I think of real friends, they are flesh and blood people: family, neighbors, mentors, colleagues. People I've seen, spoken with on more than one occasion, who's world view I know and appreciate. I carry the living memory of their eyes, voice, gestures, creativity, imagination, and place on the front lines of struggle. A friend, to me, is someone I can count on in a difficult situation, someone to whose aid I would come at a moment's notice.

I remember an era of three-cent postage stamps, letters that took months to travel by ship from one continent to another, telegraphed messages—cables, we called them—and rotary telephones on which you might make a long-distance call, but only to report a birth or death. I can still hear the staccato sound of the keys on my old Royal portable, imagine touching its smooth little plastic-covered half-moon keys, smell the lightly oiled scent of its matte metal frame, feel how the paper slipped beneath the cross bar and disappeared around the hard rubber platen. My body remembers the emphatic decision of its carriage return. My fingers have never entirely recovered from the smudge of carbon paper and messiness of whiteout.

Writing was hard work back then. It still is, but now I am freer to concentrate on the essence. Automatic page numbering, spellcheck, and cut-and-paste have largely replaced drudgery. I can store my poems in my computer, taking care to save them on something called *the cloud* as well, because even these digital marvels can crash and lose a book in progress. It's a new world. And I'm grateful for every technological advance and those yet to come.

But leave friendship out of it. I just don't warm to the idea that a perfect stranger may become a friend simply by requesting the status. I've had to *defriend* more than one person after reading a post that goes against everything I believe. A friend, to me, is still a beloved being, member of an honored category, a relationship born of shared experience and values.

Figure 5

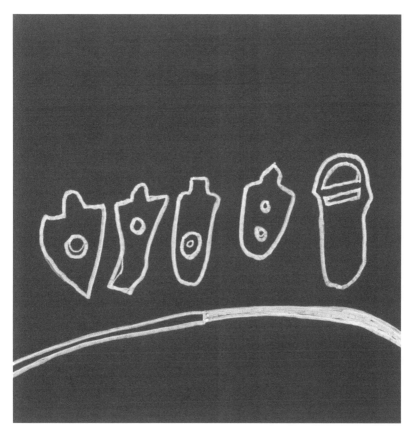

Figure 6

Bad Words

Each era's self-proclaimed guardians of language tell us some words are bad. They should not be uttered. Today those guardians are parents warning their children, teachers correcting their students, and the institutions regulating what may be said in films and the media and deciding how old you must be to listen. In public company, disapproving looks are sure to greet *a dirty mouth*. The threat: *I'll wash your mouth out with soap!* resonates with many. Even for those who never experienced that punishment, it's a vivid image. But the real problem is censorship, sponsored by systems and their institutions and invariably leading to self-censorship which is the fear of proclaiming the real you. As I write censorship of important books is at an all-time high in what have come to be known as the "red states," those where local officials believe it is their prerogative to deny children the literary experiences they need.

Although the list of bad words has changed over time, these are often those that have come to be thought of as swear words: *God-dammit, shit, fuck, asshole*. Some are slang for bodily functions; others take the name of a presumed God in vain. Words such as *slut, cunt, whore, lezzie, old maid*, and *hag* reflect our society's disrespect for women and for the process of aging. *Nigger, monkey, kike, coolie, dago, greaser, beaner, fag, raghead, pinhead, gimp, redneck, idiot,* and *white trash* support the Eurocentric, heteronormative, racist, classist, and ableist attitudes that have for so long been the underpinnings of mainstream America's narrow idea of normalcy. We are a society that clings to privilege as if it were a lifeboat to which we believe we have divine access.

The so-called bad words often appear in jokes. If we repeat them, or laugh when they are told by others, we miss an opportunity to challenge their legitimacy. *It's just a joke* or *You know I didn't mean that* won't put things right.

Who decides which words are bad and which good?

All major religions approve certain words and reject others to promote their worldview. They all have a shameful history of warfare—even genocide—against those who refuse to follow their language guidelines. The Christian crusades, misogynistic Jewish prayers, and fundamentalist Muslim hysteria about the language used to describe its prophet Mohammed, are just three examples that come to mind. Galileo Galilei suffered house arrest over the words *motion* and *inertia*, which threatened the power of the 17th century Vatican.

Dictatorial governments may declare certain words illegal; using them puts you at risk for punishment. Several Latin American dictatorships in the 1970s and '80s prohibited the use of words such as *solidarity, struggle, comrade*, as well as the names of revolutionary organizations. At the height of the COVID crisis, Donald Trump devised such a list for the United States Centers for Disease Control (CDC). Those designing the materials intended to help us handle the pandemic were told not to use the following seven terms: *vulnerable, entitlement, diversity, transgender, fetus, evidence-based* and *science-based*. With this prohibition, Trump hoped to shift the conversation away from the urgent needs of the population and toward a state of deception that would favor his authority. Eventually he was voted out of office and institutions such as the CDC tried to find their way back to a more reasonable time. But the residue of such linguistic control inevitably lingers, sometimes for generations.

I can remember when torture was considered unacceptable by almost everyone. It only took a few so-called experts reimagining the word for the act itself to become acceptable in certain circumstances. *Liberal* has gone from a descriptive political term to an insult. *Critical race theory* was once a philosophical category; now it has become subversive. Terms such as *pro-life* have gained currency today; those who identify as *pro-life* present themselves as supporters of life although they only care about the lives of fetuses, not those of living women and girls.

Words that are lies, if repeated enough, become truths to those bombarded by their din. Words that are prohibited out of some puritanical attitude toward language only reinforce a skewed sense of values.

Meanwhile, there are words that really are bad, by any moral or ethical standard. Racial slurs, terms meant to belittle and shame, and combinations like *necessary evil, deaf and dumb, collateral damage, inferior race*, and *little woman*. No evil is necessary, no damage to life is collateral, no race is inferior to another, and women are not inherently little. We often repeat these adjectives unconsciously, unaware of the ways in which they shape us going forward.

Victims of domestic abuse are often told to *keep our little secret*, thereby shifting the meaning of *secret* from something delicious to something abhorrent, repugnant, and dangerous. Daniel Ortega, the current president of Nicaragua, for nineteen years told his stepdaughter Zoilamérica that it was her revolutionary duty to submit to his sexual abuse, thus denigrating the word *revolutionary*. Wars distort the words *patriot, patriotism, hero, collateral,* and *survivor*. Commerce misuses the words *powerful, safe,* and *best*. Insurance companies routinely misuse the word *protect*. In fact, we can see how entire systems depend on language distortion to prioritize profit.

As a poet, I'm acutely conscious of language misuse and abuse. I struggle for every word I use to mean precisely what I intend. Yet I am as likely as the next person to fall into the trap of ignorance. It behooves us all to be on guard.

A Bad Habit

I have the bad habit of assuming others think the way I do. Especially about politics and social conventions. After all, they stand, look, and talk like me. Mutter *uhuh* rather than ask the relevant questions. Or any question at all. I tend to assume we grew up in similar families, went to the same sorts of schools, have the same friends. We met in places that still seem familiar, comfortable. We smile and gesture in the same ways: the lie of implied agreement. This is a fundamental error in judgment as well as practice.

I can't help believing most people want to feel secure: sheltered, healthy, fed. Their children attending decent schools. Work to be had. Care and solace as they age. I have trouble understanding why anyone cares about the color of my skin, whether I am a man, woman, or any other gender, whom I love, or what color I paint my house.[9] I don't really believe that okra is edible or that anyone would voluntarily choose a dessert flavor other than

---

9. I am referring here to the fact that several decades ago the writer Sandra Cisneros painted her house purple in an upscale neighborhood of San Antonio, Texas. Social pressure tried to get her to repaint it white. She resisted.

chocolate. Too much sugar keeps you running in circles. Too much fat strains your waistband.

They say that . . . was prelude to most opinions uttered by my mother. She couldn't tell you who *they* were but made the statement in an authoritative voice. Reasonable. You could fill in the blank in any number of ways. *They say the economy will get worse. They say the neighborhood is going to the dogs, property values are falling. They say it will be a nice day tomorrow. They say that the senator and his secretary . . .* It was how she positioned herself. To be thought of as intelligent, taken seriously. A recipe for acceptance, agreement, belief. She was unaware there was another way.

Another line she led with was: *Everyone knows that . . .* Again, you could finish the sentence. I remember the precise timbre of her voice. *Everyone knows carbonated drinks dissolve the enamel on your teeth. Everyone knows aspirin is bad for you. Everyone knows hand lotion is a waste of money. Everyone knows baking soda is as good as toothpaste and costs less. A broad forehead means intelligence. You can tell by looking.*

Mother's dialog openers could be low-key or shocking. Her specialty was the latter. *Well, everyone knows Jesus was gay.* She was standing before the counter at our neighborhood café, waiting to order her usual lunchtime cup of vegetable soup. We hadn't been discussing religion or iconic figures or homosexuality. The statement floated on the air and stayed, refusing to fade or dim. Others waiting in line looked at her and each other, then away. Conversations gradually resumed. I remember we also discussed the dubious benefits of computers over typewriters that day.

From an early age I knew I would be a writer. Eventually I had the courage to call myself a poet. Words were important. I would choose them carefully, arrange them in unusual ways. I wanted them to describe as accurately as possible that which I wanted them to say. No detours or doubt. Uniquely mine. I hoped all those who read my words would see the images I saw, those who heard them vibrate in the same musical register. This also meant putting first and last names to opinions, whether spoken by a well-known expert or a child.

Maybe that's why I grew careless, assuming everyone received my words the way I intended. They don't. Not only my words, anyone's words. All words. We think we are speaking the same language, but our experiences serve that language up differently. We say we respect difference.

Not true.

To Be or Not to Be

There was a time, maybe twenty or thirty years ago, when people were fond of saying *you aren't what you do but who you are*, as if it demonstrated some sort of emotional disequilibrium to think of yourself in terms of accomplishment, creating a useful product. *Just be yourself*, they said, with more than a whiff of superiority. Reaping the perks of a consumer society while appearing oblivious to its vacuity had something to do with the equation. The implication was that if you were emotionally healthy you could simply *be*. No angst about doing or producing anything.

Some of those who said this made a lot of money doing so. And yes, it was what they did. Most were male, blond, blue-eyed and with eternally youthful features. They looked the part, wore success like this year's fashion. There were books and magazine articles, conferences, retreats, therapies, how-to manuals, workshops, and Ted Talks. An industry. Today there would be podcasts as well.

This has always seemed embarrassing to me, like something you remove from your nose when you don't think anyone is looking or a smear of something gross stuck to the sole of your shoe.

I'm always doing something. Even when I'm not doing anything, that nothing is its own doing. It might be monumental in design, hope to become something of note. It might be insignificant. Sometimes it has been dangerous, presenting me with several paths from which to choose. The choosing itself is a doing.

I'm lucky to have made it through. My indolence may be fragile, disappearing before I can give it a name. And naming is an important doing, fraught with responsibility. When we name well, it can be a prelude to journeys of being and doing. When we give something a name that doesn't fit, it can lead us down the wrong path. U-turns are always costly.

I lie on the couch, letting my eyes close, mind wander. Maybe I've fallen asleep watching one of those inane Netflix specials where nothing of interest happens, but inertia keeps me from picking up the remote. Remembering can be arduous, a doing that requires every color of energy. I remember hiking La Luz trail to Sandia Crest, breathing in and out with the changing ecosystems. Remembering is an action. It can cause you to tremble, pull a thick shawl about your shoulders, or sweat until your skin glistens with invisible crystals of salt.

I am no longer able to do many of the things I once did. Hike, for instance, or ride a bike or work out at a climbing gym. Make do on four hours' sleep. Walk completely upright. Toss back a full head of hair. Wear high heels or a bra. Keep my opinions to myself. Dispense idle small talk. Pretend, for politeness or convenience's sake, that all is well with the world. *It'll be okay.* I've always regarded that as a ridiculous statement, worthy of disdain.

Remembering can get you in trouble too. Am I remembering that wrong? Am I conflating mother's green rayon dress, the one adorned with the cream-colored rope pattern, with the stubborn bark on the oak tree in front of our house? When did the man with the dark slicked-back hair come into the picture? The demarcation between that stiff mat and the whiteness of his forehead dances drunk behind my eyes. Am I inventing the story, or does it really exist?

It takes a certain courage to refrain from worrying about making as opposed to being. Perhaps it implies a conceit. You think so much of yourself that you aren't obliged to produce something useful to others. It's enough that they recognize your existence. But first you must recognize your existence. Some of us have been conditioned to have a hard time with that.

Recognizing yourself, your unique gift, your right to take up space and breathe air, requires both making and doing. We can practice in any position: vertical, on the go, in motion, or without uttering a word. And it takes practice. You must knock out a few intruders along the way. Convincing yourself and then remembering that it's true are two separate triumphs.

They can support or cancel each other out.

You only know whether you've lived a productive life if you learn to remember and practice the skill. Then you must try not to forget the remembering.

Figure 7

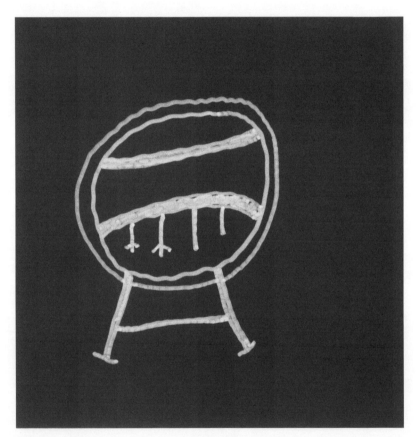

Figure 8

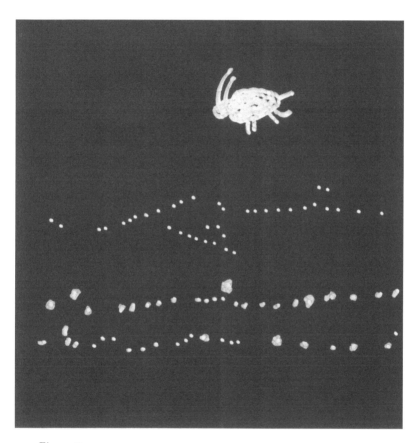

Figure 9

Fanatic vs. Writer

"Respect for religion has become a code phrase meaning "fear of religion." Religion, like all other ideas, deserve criticism, satire, and yes, our fearless disrespect."
    —Salmon Rushdie

Freedom to express one's ideas, no matter how they may differ from government rhetoric, religious dogma, or mainstream sentiment, is one of the guarantees upon which our nation was founded. Nothing is more elementary or precious than freedom of expression. We take it for granted here and vigorously protest its suppression in other countries.

I know something about this issue. In 1984, after living outside the United States for almost a quarter century, I came home. Having acquired Mexican citizenship when married to a Mexican two decades before, I'd inadvertently lost my US status and had to apply for residency. My application was denied based on opinions expressed in seven of my books. With a support system made up of thousands of people who understood freedom of expression to be an inalienable right, I won my case in 1989. With a stroke of the legal system's pen, I regained my citizenship and was able to live in the land of my birth, close to my aging parents, and on the high desert landscape I love.

But not before having been the target of death threats. An angry young man beat me up one day in my office at the University of New Mexico, leading to a campus detective having to be posted outside my door each time I conferred with students. I received ugly letters and calls. In one, the writer promised he would: *cut you end to end and pour lye into your vagina.* Strangers rushing me on the street might be offering a hug or wielding a weapon. I almost crashed my car when the occupants of another vehicle followed me on a high-velocity freeway, flaunting a hastily hand-drawn sign that said: *Pinko, go back where you came from.* The irony is that I come from here. For almost five years I lived with the stress of constant vigilance.

Now, more than thirty years later, a much more brutal assault on freedom of expression revives the feelings of fear and insecurity produced by those attacks. On August 12, 2022, Salman Rushdie had just taken his place on stage at the Chautauqua Institute in western New York state. He was about the give a talk about *the United States as a haven for exiled writers.* An enraged 24-year-old named Hadi Matar rushed the writer, stabbing him multiple times in the neck, arm, and torso. He also managed to hurt the event's moderator. Before the assailant could be stopped and Rushdie rescued, the latter had sustained serious injuries. As I write, he is on a ventilator, cannot speak, is expected to lose one eye and the use of his arm, and his liver is seriously damaged.[10]

This attack responds to a 1989 fatwa issued by Iran's Supreme Leader, Ayatollah Ruhollah Khomeini, in response to Rushdie's novel *The Satanic Verses.* The book fictionalizes parts of the Prophet Muhammad's life, and the religious authorities weren't happy with the depiction. Fundamentalists of all faiths distinguish what they believe to be *the word of God* from

---

10. Rushdie did survive but required a long healing process and lost an eye.

metaphor, fiction, or any secular text. Khomeini's fatwa ordered all Muslims to kill Rushdie for the crime of blasphemy. A price of several million dollars was put on the writer's head. As of 2012, an Iranian religious foundation had raised the bounty to a total of $3.3 million.

Many people have died in demonstrations protesting the novel's publication, including twelve in a riot in Mumbai in February 1989 and six more in another riot in Islamabad that same year. Copies of the book have been burned, and there have been attacks on bookstores. Anyone connected to the book risks violence.

For several decades, the author of *The Satanic Verses* lived in fear for his life. He spent years in hiding in London, protected by the British police. His situation was made more dramatic when, in 1991, the novel's Japanese translator Hitoshi Igarashi was stabbed to death and its Italian translator Ettore Capriolo badly wounded. Two years later, the novel's Norwegian publisher William Nygaard was shot three times outside his home in Oslo. He was seriously hurt but survived.

Gradually, the apparent cessation of such incidents gave Rushdie a false sense of security. He began to reappear in public, saying: *I must live my life.* I can sympathize with his feeling that he could return to some semblance of normalcy. We tend to isolate our own experience from popular manifestations of racism and hate, not realizing that these attitudes have increased manyfold in recent years.

But fanatics don't forget.

As the Davids of this world confront the Goliaths, *speaking truth to power* has become a mandate that both describes our stance and is meant to imbue us with the courage to stand up for what we believe, despite the forces lined up against us. Many of us have grown up with the ditty *Sticks and stones may break my bones, but words will never hurt me.* The saying is thought to have first appeared in *The Christian Recorder* of March 1862, a publication of the African Methodist Episcopal Church, or AME. Like so many nursery rhymes, it is misleading.

In fact, words are powerful. These murders and other attacks show just how much so.

But the real, lasting, power resides in the words themselves: creations of intelligence and imagination that keep us alert to dogma and the deadening influence of follow-the-leader language.

Lies

I still remember my astonishment when Carol, one of my two best friends in high school, casually mentioned she'd told a lie. We must have been around fifteen. I no longer remember the context or what the lie was. It was her offhand confession that produced a memory that still itches. I lied about all sorts of things but would never have admitted doing so. The social mores of the times taught me not to.

Lying was verbally discouraged in my childhood home. My parents constantly lauded the virtues of honesty. *It's the best policy* they always said. But they lied easily and often. In response to my insistent questions, they said they'd changed our surname from Reinthal to Randall *because it was easier to spell.* My mother was stricken with breast cancer when the disease was still something you didn't talk about. For the rest of her long life, she claimed she wrenched her lymph-swollen arm while driving. Her extramarital affairs also had to be carefully hidden. The well-worn path through foothill underbrush to the home of one of her lovers must have been made by the repeated trek of some large animal.

Unearned money, inherited from our father's family, was embarrassing in their class and culture. It was explained away as what our parents saved by serving horsemeat and bloody eggs or substituting 50-pound kegs of powdered milk for the bottles of whole milk delivered to our neighbor's door. It was because of that judicious thriftiness that we were able to take exotic summer trips, they said. And I grew up repeating those lies until I was old enough to realize how absurd they sounded.

Of course, there were different degrees of falsehoods: from those that showcased an entirely invented life story or could land you in trouble with the law to the *little white lie* considered inoffensive, even expected in polite society. We never questioned why those socially acceptable lies were called white. Nor did we assign a color to the big ones. How are you today? *Fine, thank you*, is still the automatic response (although you might in fact be broke or depressed or sick). How are the kids? *Doing well* (although the oldest might have a heroin habit and the youngest just failed algebra). The readymade lie is especially egregious when applied to someone else. A friend has just been diagnosed with a terminal illness and you hasten to assure her *everything will be all right*. This sort of response is supposed to give her hope. Increasingly it gives me pause.

And then there are people we call pathological liars, those compelled to lie about everything all the time. *Pathological liar* is a term we use without really knowing if it is a pathology in the scientific sense. I won't pretend to understand the condition. But I wonder if some aren't more in tune with this hypocritical culture than we care to admit. I wonder, too, if all pathological liars are motivated by a personal disequilibrium. Some may exhibit *the etiquette of poverty*, as Joshua Hunt writes, "a means of getting by for the poor, and a gift we give to the rich; and a practice that lets us avoid talking about the uncomfortable difference between us. Observing this etiquette doesn't feel dishonest because its falsehood recognizes the deeper truth that many of society's institutions are hostile to the poor. Lying to the landlord keeps a roof over our head. Lying to the social worker keeps our family together. Lying to Immigration keeps a family member from deportation. Lying to ourselves allows us to believe it's all going to be OK, somehow, someday. That kind of lying is not so much learned as imposed."[11]

As I got older, I came to understand that our entire social fabric is woven of lies. Denial was always at the ready: George Washington is said to have admitted that he did in fact cut down that cherry tree. Abraham Lincoln was known as Honest Abe. Yet every thinking person, if asked, would have to admit that our early European settlers lied to the Indians when they forced them into treaties that robbed them of their homelands or passed out those bottles of whiskey and small-pox-infested blankets. It wasn't only a lie, but brutally offensive, to claim that kidnapped slaves were content working for their *kind masters.* There was something historically wrong with describing the bombing of Hiroshima and Nagasaki as *saving lives. Immigrants take American jobs, Guns don't kill, people do,* and *Life begins at conception,* are but three of the current lies designed to confuse and confound. Recent electoral processes have documented such ploys as *If you didn't vote today, you can always do so tomorrow,* a lie aimed at preventing certain groups from casting their ballots.

We remember George W. Bush's lie about Iraq possessing weapons of mass destruction. A secretary of state known for his honesty[12] was forced to stand up in Congress waving the fabricated proof. This was the lie that justified our invasion of that oil-rich country, causing the deaths of tens of thousands on both sides and the destruction of artistic and scientific treasures that belonged to all of humanity. The lie soon unraveled, but by then we were fully engaged in the military operation and *had to finish what we'd started.* It seems it's always more expedient to lie first and explain or apologize later.

Each time we hold elections, we know the candidates lie. They lie about what they will do if they win. And they lie about their opponents, hoping

---

11. "How I Became a Pathological Liar," New York Times, July 13, 2022.
12. Colin Luther Powell, 1937-2021.

to cripple their chances. The truth may emerge later, but by then the damage has been done. Perhaps the greatest political lie in recent times was the one Donald Trump told when he insisted that he'd won the 2020 presidential election. Despite all evidence to the contrary, *Stop the Steal* was the catchy phrase he coined to get people to believe Biden had lost. Long past coercions, recounts, and unsuccessful legal challenges, he just kept making the claim—proving that if you repeat something often enough it will become a sort of post-modern truth. When that failed, he orchestrated an attack on the US Capitol in a desperate attempt to stay in office. His supporters aren't put off by his dishonesty; they see it as necessary to achieving their political goals.

There are times when lying may in fact be justified. We are not ashamed of lying to the people and institutions that would destroy us and those we love. Because I have spent my life fighting for justice, I have often told such lies. Yet I was shocked when forces I still considered revolutionary strayed from the truth. When international Communism led us to believe that the Cambodian genocide was an invention of Western journalists, I briefly believed the fabrication. Discovering the terrible truth put an end to my follow-the-leader mentality and caused me to question every subsequent dictate, independent of its source.

Our media, once known for its impartiality, lies when profit is at stake. The brave journalist who told the truth is mostly a figure of the past, worthy of a book or film. All our major religions lie about their scriptures being *The Word of God*. For years, the Catholic Church maintained its priests had never sexually abused their congregants and that bishops hadn't covered up the crimes. Whistleblowers, once considered courageous, now know they will be fired or worse before they can get the word out. Daniel Ellsberg was a hero; thirty years later Edward Snowden is a criminal.

Supposedly serious research studies sponsored by companies selling medications and foodstuffs routinely lie about their findings. Corporate advertising lies about its products. Several candidates lied under oath during their congressional nomination hearings, assuring themselves lifetime appointments to the Supreme Court. Now they lie about what was written into the Constitution and how what they claim our founders meant should regulate our lives today. We need only look at the lies spread during the worst of the COVID-19 pandemic to understand how they may send otherwise informed people in the wrong direction, costing millions of lives.

Meanwhile, we continue to publicly applaud honesty and tell each other we are a truth-telling nation. After all, Americans are known for being outspoken, guileless, direct. Transparency is our middle name. Not too long ago, the Seven Pillars of Character, a lesson taught in our public schools, encouraged *Caring, Courage, Citizenship, Respect, Responsibility, Honesty, and Fairness.* Despite the extreme mixed message it sent, teachers were required to expound on these virtues in every grade.

Sometimes I think about my high school friend and wonder at her ability to be honest about dishonesty. She was a step ahead of the rest of us.

Fat

The word itself is an insult: *You're fat. Fatso.* There are societies, I'm thinking of Cuba, where fat—*gorda*—is an endearment denoting health and therefore beauty. Traditionally, only the wealthy could eat well, and a robust constitution was considered beautiful. The revolution changed that, but the label remains. In most cultures, though, fat is not a compliment. It implies revulsion and induces shame. For women, especially, the thinner the better. But wait, not too thin. Anorexia and bulimia are also shameful conditions to be kept behind closed doors.

The fashion industry hangs its clothes on the slimmest bodies. Models starve themselves to keep their jobs. The direction of stripes, hemlengths, shoulders, pleats, tucks, belts, and waistlines are all designed to make us appear thinner than we are. It wasn't that long ago that airline stewardesses had to keep their weight below a specified level. Even today, a slim woman will be hired over a full-bodied one every time. Zero dress size is the goal.

A boy can be bullied for being fat and chided for overweight as an adult. But a beer belly speaks camaraderie, good times. An overweight girl can only be miserable: criticized, teased, unwanted. Shaming is always bad. Some feminists have coined the term *fat shaming* and claim that *fat is beautiful.* They're right about the shaming part. But they often refuse to acknowledge the health hazards inherent to being overweight. The Centers for Disease Control (CDC) say that from 1999 to 2017 US obesity prevalence in the United States increased from 30.5% to 41.9%, with severe obesity rising from 4.7% to 9.2%. Obesity-related conditions include heart disease, stroke, type 2 diabetes, and certain cancers. Not to mention the fact that extra weight may cause accidents. On average, medical costs for adults with obesity are almost $2,000 dollars more a year than for those with a healthy weight. Fat may be beautiful, but it can kill.

Like so much social stigma, cause is ignored while its effects are treated like outcomes you can avoid if you only try. *Just try harder! Where is your willpower?* Weight problems for many women come from childhood sexual abuse. Some women clothe themselves in extra poundage so that men won't treat them like objects of desire. Working to heal the origin of the problem would undoubtedly bring better results than remedies that only attack the image.

There is also an economic component to healthy eating, and as the rich get richer and poor poorer, more people are affected by its restraints. Processed foods, with their fat-producing ingredients, cost a fraction of what a single peach or bell pepper will set you back. A single mother of four is more able to treat her kids to calorie-packed hamburgers than to healthy salads. *Soft Serve* is too often the desert of choice.

For her entire adult life, my mother weighed around 110 pounds. She would tell me I should lose weight, then tempt me with a special desert. From a young age, I was burdened by the struggle to control my weight, until a series of events changed everything. First, I fell in love with my partner of 37 years. She introduced me to biking and hiking. I knew I would have to limber up to enjoy those sports and decided to get in shape. Regular visits to a gym helped me shed some excess weight. But writing is a sedentary lifestyle, and I didn't really get thin. A couple of decades later, my body itself rebelled. If I wasn't going to stop overeating, it would make the necessary adjustments for me. Without dieting, I simply stopped eating what I didn't need. In my case, smaller portions and regular exercise keeps the unwanted weight off. I'm only sharing my experience, not offering it as a recipe to others.

Diets themselves are to blame for much of the weight we carry. Weight-watchers, Nutra-System, Atkins, Paleo, Mayo Clinic, Mediterranean, South Beach, and Intermittent Fasting, among others. Each advertises itself as the latest miracle. Celebrities are paid for their testimonies which desperate women believe. Pay a modest monthly fee, and the individually wrapped meals will arrive at your door. Be disciplined and consistent. But the outcome is almost invariably the same. You will lose weight and then gain it back plus something extra, and the brand exploiting you will profit from your disappointment. You will celebrate, then despair, and go through it all again. And again. Too many women repeat the cycle throughout their lives, forever hoping next time will be the charm. Some even swear by plans that have failed them, like obsessive gamblers who talk about their wins but never their losses—except that dieters talk about their losses rather than their gains.

When diets fail, obese women often resort to surgery. There are options: gastric bypass, sleeve gastrectomy, adjustable gastric band, biliopancreatic diversion with duodenal switch, among others. All carry risks and produce uncomfortable or unpleasant side-effects. Thinness is such a pervasive goal in many western societies that women who have not been able to lose weight any other way subject themselves to any solution they believe may work for them.

Body weight has become a complicated issue in our culture. I know I haven't written the final word on how it haunts us. For now, though, I'll say one thing: It's your life. We're given one body and it's up to each of us to make of it what we will.

Pride

I t starts when we're very young. Or doesn't. A parent or teacher says they're proud of us for a perceived accomplishment. It might be anything from mastering the natural evolution of walking or uttering our first word, to fighting back or not fighting back when teased or bullied. Boys typically receive praise for aggressive behavior, girls for docility or simply for being pretty or thin. Sometimes our elders tell us they are proud of us for something that is inappropriate or even dangerous. Sometimes we never get the praise we deserve.

There are children who never hear the words *I'm proud of you* and spend their lives working in vain to earn them from a parent long dead. Some—often boys—hear them so often that they grow up believing themselves capable of anything, a purveyor of male entitlement that has skewed our power relations. In our misogynist society, girls and women are rarely praised for displaying independence; shame becomes an expected place for us to dwell.

National pride always runs the risk of going off the rails and becoming the sort of nationalism that can morph into a neo-fascist sense of superiority. In the United States we tell members of our armed forces that we are proud of them and back the compliment up with medals, parades, special discounts, monuments, gold stars in windows, and military funerals. *Thank you for your service* is a phrase you're likely to hear just about anywhere: in airports, supermarkets, or on the street. This is a pride that doesn't concern itself with whether a particular war is just. We want our fighting men and women to know their sacrifice is appreciated; governmental lies, imperialist policy, disrespect for the sovereignty of other nations, racism, and wanton cruelty be damned.

And this is a complicated issue. I don't want to confuse an individual's sacrifice with a policy that used him or her as cannon fodder. I know soldiers' personal stories rarely have anything to do with the forces that put them in danger. They may come from a military family, enlist because a distorted sense of patriotism leads them to believe it is their duty, or because it means a job. I can be proud of the individual fighter even when I deplore the war that took him thousands of miles from home and pitted him against other fighters with other cultures who speak other languages and, in most cases, are simply defending their homes. Still, I have never been able to tell a man or woman in uniform: *Thank you for your service.*

This issue reached crisis proportions in my lifetime during the US American war in Vietnam. Increasingly, that war challenged our sense of right and wrong. Young people waged a protest movement powerful enough to turn the tide. Tens of thousands of soldiers refused the draft or deserted. And when those who did serve came home, they weren't met with the ticker-tape parades that had greeted veterans of previous wars. The pride wasn't there. But neither was the understanding or compassion. In antiwar demonstrations, anger was often directed at those who fought instead of those who made the policy. I opposed the war but never felt I wanted to aim my anger at individual soldiers. They had suffered enough. Home country rejection only added to the trauma that would accompany many for the rest of their lives.

How do you parse pride so that the emotion is sincere even when the larger picture is murky? A nation's pride and where it is directed requires informed analysis, the sort of public conversation rarely encouraged here. It also requires kindness.

Many discriminated-against groups have used the word *pride* to claim their rightful place in society. Native Pride. Black Pride. Latinx Pride. Gay Pride. The LGBQT+ community has long used the term to describe the exuberant parades held in June of each year, in which people at any point on the gender arc and our allies come out, often in flamboyant costume, to say: *We are here, and we are proud.* In this context, by publicly claiming pride in our identities we are rebelling against the shame imposed upon us by a racist, misogynist, or heteronormative mainstream.

Indeed, shame and pride are opposites, whether expressed nationally or by a group or individual. Just as pride may run the gamut from the legitimate satisfaction of a job well done to a false sense of importance when the values are off, shame may range from the momentary response about a minor misunderstanding to an overriding emotion that consumes your life and shapes who you become. When racial and sexual minorities only saw themselves represented on film and in the media as incidental, token, comic relief, or criminals, it promoted a communal shame that has been difficult to overcome. As minorities began to be depicted as whole human beings, that shame started to dissolve. Assumptions such as *your skirt was too short* or *if you work hard enough, you'll get ahead* are no longer immune to challenge.

Studies have shown that the shame of having suffered childhood sexual abuse and the trauma that ensues is analogous to the shame an entire country suffers when its citizens haven't been able to prevent a genocide or some other national crime. We remember Germany, South Africa, Cambodia, Chile. At different moments in history and depending on their cultures, people have faced these traumas differently. Truth and Reconciliation commissions have worked best when they have taken unique conditions and cultures into account.

In every instance, working through the shame requires first naming and placing the blame on those responsible, acknowledging the damage they have done, exploring its ramifications, and resolving its repercussions in ways that are fair to circumstance as well as victim. Interestingly, the recovery movement of the 1980s and '90s initiated this important work. It, in turn, influenced the way we think about the trauma of war and other public catastrophes. Feminism enabled us to reimagine power and has been central to this process. Rather than the broad political panorama informing our personal lives, it has been the other way around; insights about intimate relationships have helped us think about the larger political struggles.

Today we live in a world in which shame and pride still too often find themselves in unequal relation. The right is proud of stripping women and minorities of their rights. The mainstream left is still more than a few steps behind in recognizing how serious and well organized our opponents are. It has been arrogant when it should have been humble, lax when it would have been better to be determined. Shame is not an emotion I wish on anyone. But pride must be reserved for those attitudes and actions that bring respect and healing to all.

Figure 10

Fear

ear has many faces. There is that fear that counsels us against situations that may bring us harm. We call this a useful fear. We are too close to a fire and the heat from its flames prompts us to step back. Walking along a precipitous mountain trail, a shudder strangles our breath, steering us safely away from its edge. A *Beware of Dog* sign tells us not to stick our hand through a wire fence. The game looks dangerous; self-preservation says don't become a player. A stranger's questions are too inquisitive; better to smile and turn away. Another's story is a warning. These and many other fears are cautionary tales, keeping us from danger.

Then there is the phobia, a fear worse than fear and of an entirely different quality. If you are not possessed by one, you cannot imagine its terror. This is an imposter fear, pretending to be what it's not and worse by uncountable factors. Spiders. Snakes. Heights. I once knew someone who was terrified of the flower called Black-Eyed Susan. They often grow wild along country roads, a golden ribbon admired by many. Who knows what they represented to her?

I am plagued by a phobia of mushrooms. I cannot let them near me, can't even look at them in photographs, sometimes dream I must navigate a narrowing path where they are closing in on either side. There is no escape.

Every one of my body's orifices snaps shut and still I am doomed. From earliest childhood, I sought and developed ways to avoid their threat. I said *no thanks* to picnics, used only paved pathways in the park, avoided the supermarket produce aisle. In mid-life I learned that the origin of my phobia was incest perpetrated by my maternal grandparents. He raped me while she watched. I retrieved the memory in therapy. Knowing its source has helped me understand my life but hasn't liberated me from its horror.

There are those who claim they are afraid of nothing. The declaration itself is evidence of fear, hiding behind a mask of bravado. A veteran of many battles once told me that anyone who says they are not afraid when facing enemy fire is lying. In the US we inhabit a culture that is more afraid of the National Rifle Association than it is of psychopaths owning a gun. Or several guns. Or assault weapons designed for war. They demand protection of those rights although they know they facilitate the repeated massacres of young schoolchildren, their devoted teachers, and unsuspecting citizens going about the everyday business of living. We are afraid of a Supreme Court majority that has returned women to second-class citizenry, effectively rendering us chattel.

All animals have built-in fear monitors that tell them danger is near, when it's too hot or too cold, when to dress themselves in camouflage, when to run and when to fight. Human animals are born with these detectors as well, but eons of conditioning have created devious obstacles, dulled our senses, and invented false stories that dilute our intuition. We've become the only animal that can be tricked by the lies.

Patriarchy nurtures a fear in women unlike any other. It smiles sweetly. It is a fear too many women express in moments of daily subjugation: walking a few steps behind, the willing hands, the upturned eyes, the fluttering lashes, the adoring sigh, and the automatic *yes*. In short, the tyranny of another's gluttony over our own needs. Agreement even before demand reaches full volume. Submission comes from the dread of growing old alone, of not being validated by the gender we are conditioned to believe superior, and it becomes its own brand of fear.

There is another sort of fear, the kind created by a person or institution for which fear is a useful weapon of manipulation and control. Intentionally, out of pure malice, or unconsciously because the culture encourages such deception. *Father knows best. Driving while Black. The police are there to protect us. Disobey God's law and hell awaits,* complete with its eternity of fire and brimstone. Your husband or boyfriend tells you if you leave, he will kill you. *A good child obeys. A good student doesn't ask questions. The doctor knows best. A real patriot goes to war.* Such traps weave a cacophony that distorts memory, silences wisdom, and makes it impossible to follow our own instincts. It crushes our spirit and turns us into prey.

I was afraid of what lay behind the trap door in the ceiling of my early childhood closet.

I was afraid of allowing anyone to discover my secrets and use them against me.

I was afraid of being a wallflower forever.

I was afraid of social suffocation.

I was afraid of a charging elephant on the ridge above Tanzania's Tarangire valley.

I was afraid on the Serengeti plains of the ominous nighttime growls the nearby lion pride emitted as it devoured its kill.

I was afraid of the lies told by mediocre bureaucrats exercising their quotas of power.

I was afraid of a sociopathic president.

I am afraid of fascism.

I am afraid something may happen to those I love.

I am afraid of myself when I am afraid.

Time

Time tells the unschooled observer that it runs consecutively, a linear measure we use to describe the length of a movement through space, our finite life on earth for instance. But I don't believe it's that simple. Our relationship to time's progression is different, depending on who and where we are and what is happening around us. It may stretch or compress that progression, nudging it toward anxiety, loneliness, illness, numbness, or sudden joy. It may grow tentacles that clutch and squeeze our heart or drag it toward a twilight of indifference. Discrete cultures shape time differently, as do class, gender, race, and other variables. From earliest history, we have wondered about the possibility of simultaneous universes, time-bending, and other surprises.

The above is a poet's musing. Were I a scientist, I might have a more complex or evidence-based definition. New ideas about time are being explored constantly. I have just read an article about tachyons that describes a hypothetical particle that moves faster than the speed of light and thus travels backwards through time.[13] The article claims that

---

13. Tachyons: Facts about these faster-than-light particles," by Robert Lea in Space .com, November 24, 2021.

tachyons aren't just science fiction but the stuff of hard science. The idea is based on Einstein's 1905 theory of special relativity which postulates that nothing with mass moves faster than the speed of light and that physical laws remain the same in all non-inertial reference frames. This leads to the understanding that space and time are united in a single entity: spacetime.

When the poet applies her imagination to spacetime, she may link the cosmically powerful and violent, like the supernova explosion of a distant star and the mundane, such as an egg dropping, cracking open and spattering on the floor. The proverbial flutter of a butterfly's wings and a weather event halfway around the world. Such phenomena can be mapped onto a spacetime diagram, in other words the connection can be demonstrated, at least on paper. The article concludes that tachyons reveal the importance of imagination in our ongoing quest to understand the universe. Our curiosity may capture what our technology can't yet. We can consider the possibility of a particle that journeys back through time and what that says about the nature of time itself.

Time seems to move at a different pace when we're old than it did when we were young. The very evidence of age—how it changes our skin, hair, teeth, eyes, muscle mass—is dramatic when we're seven contemplating parents in their thirties. By the time we ourselves are thirty or forty—or eighty—we tend to see age in new ways. And not necessarily uniformly. Now in my nineth decade, I feel ancient in some ways and younger than ever in others.

The concept of age has changed with the passage of centuries. Thousands of years ago, people could reasonably expect to live into their twenties or thirties. Even going back hundreds of years, before the invention of antibiotics, diseases that are now curable carried young people off. When I was a child, life expectancy in the United States was in the low sixties, slightly longer for women than for men. Today it isn't that unusual to live to be 90, and increasing numbers reach 100 or more. But these statistics are only relevant for those who have dependable shelter, enough to eat and access to medical care. Populations denied such rights die sooner and often in ways that elemental justice can prevent.

We must also deal with what I call knotted time, a sudden cluster or parenthesis in which a misunderstanding with someone we love disrupts a few hours or days like a poison wind pushing waves against an eroding coastline. The surf is pounding in your ears, filling your mouth, threatening to pull your breastbone through your skin—all under water in a state akin to drowning. Time is neither moving forward nor back but engaged in a paralyzing frenzy that upends direction. What remains is a garment turned inside out, its torn lining visible to the world.

The COVID-19 pandemic altered time for many of us. We couldn't work or socialize as we had. Enforced quarantine, the inability to follow our usual rhythms and adopt a more deliberative way of moving through the average day, all seemed to conspire to slow time dramatically. For people living alone or who were particularly vulnerable for one reason or another, time weighed more. I am fortunate to live with a loving partner and be able to work online, so my inner clock wasn't as affected. I even experienced some benefits: I found I was cooking more slowly and carefully, which enhanced the quality of the food I prepared. I found myself revising my poems more, which also made them better. The slowdown produced a new sense of focus. But I was also affected in ways I have yet to understand.

There are moments in every life when time escapes consciousness. This can happen when a child suffers physical or sexual abuse. Disassociation removes the abuse from memory, leaving a gaping hole in the jigsaw puzzle of her calendar. Successful therapy may retrieve that memory, restoring the picture to sequence and continuity. But time is always altered.

Any traumatic or monumental experience may result in similar distortion. This happens with labor and childbirth. Both are wrenchingly painful but going through them wipes visceral memory. We remember the fact of the pain but cannot consciously recreate it. I vividly recall each time I gave birth but am unable to conjure the discomfort. Were this erasure not part of the experience, women might not bear more than a single child.

Do wrongly condemned prisoners ever get back their time behind bars? When an injustice is remedied many years later, does the time elapsed disappear? I am thinking of Leonard Peltier and others, who have spent decades in prison for crimes they didn't commit. What do a few seconds, minutes, or days mean to those enduring torture and hoping to be able to resist until their comrades have had a chance to abandon safe houses, destroy evidence, move resources, escape?

I also think of Jim Thorpe, stripped of his 1912 Olympic gold medal in that year's decathlon and pentathlon. The honor wasn't restored until 2022, long after Thorpe himself had died. Or the medals won at the 1968 Olympic games by Tommie Smith and Juan Carlos. Smith and Carlos raised their black-gloved fists during the playing of the Star-Spangled Banner in protest over South African apartheid and racism within the Olympic movement. They finally received their medals in 2016. What became of the time between win and reward?

During Senator Joseph McCarthy's Anti-Communist witch hunt of the 1950s, many Hollywood screenwriters and actors, teachers, and others lost their jobs. Those who were finally readmitted to their professions, survived years of silencing without the possibility of working or supporting themselves and their families. All these repressive periods left holes in lives, altering them irrevocably. Did those years disappear or are they reflected in mirrors that speak a language we are still trying to decipher?

I have a daughter who sets her clock eighteen minutes ahead. This helps her to be on time. Do those eighteen minutes exist in some alternative space, or are they simply erased by her gesture? I too run my wristwatch five minutes fast, convincing myself I may make that connecting flight on time. *Killing time* is a popular expression that reflects the opposite of what it describes. It should never be taken literally.

When a bad relationship ends, one that was abusive to one or both partners, what happens to those years of misery? Do they become a lesson learned or will they be repeated in another guise? What happens to the years cut from a life? Where does time go when it collapses? And what about a time lived to its fullest? Is it magnified?

And there is the greater picture: Without going so far as to contemplate the existence of tachyons, I look at time trapped for 1.84 billion years in the polished gneiss of Grand Canyon or etched into the rings of a millennial tree. Time examined by archaeologists in an ear of corn chewed clean and dried for hundreds of years or contained in a clay pot half hidden in desert sand. Time measured by the scientist in the long core of ice carefully raised from a depth of eight thousand feet, bearing a message from the last ice age. Secrets dancing in a bubble of air, a *time capsule* supreme.

In 1976, the installation artist Donald Judd wrote: *Any time that you think of is only the relation or sequence of events, how long a person lives, human biology, or how many times the earth goes around the sun (. . .).* Makes sense to me.

Heat

Temperature determines a great deal. If our body temperature reaches or rises above 105 degrees Fahrenheit, we risk irreversible damage to our organs, including our brains. Our minds may travel to a place from which there is no return. We have coined the phrase *global warming* as an ever-hotter planet threatens us with extreme weather events, ferocious storms, devastating fires, melting ice caps, eroding coastlines, and island nations disappearing into the sea. As I write, London is experiencing the hottest temperature in recorded history and crops in southern Europe are withering in the fields. To stop this slow-motion burning at the stake of humanity and our habitats, we would have to seriously reduce our use of fossil fuels, something we have so far only been willing to talk about, not do. As with so many life and death issues, we continue our mad race to oblivion—accompanied by unconvincing language, non-binding agreements, and broken promises.

Literal burning at the stake was a form of capital punishment popular during the Middle Ages and even beyond. It was often reserved for those perceived to be heretics: nonbelievers in the dogma of the day, witches, and scientists. Although all genders were targeted, women were the prime victims. Joan of Arc met her death in this way, and many point to her submitting to the punishment rather than denouncing her military campaign as proof of her faith.

Hot under the collar was an expression I heard my father say, often uttered in the generation before my own. It was almost always directed at someone else or used to describe a person who was upset about some minor transgression. The implication was that staying calm would have been the better course—*cooling down*, to use the opposite metaphor.

Heat is also associated with sexuality, human or animal: *a hot love scene* or *a dog in heat*. *Burning desire* is intense longing. A *hot date* means your partner is sexy. There is nothing subtle about the description. You imagine panting and sweating.

"There'll Be a Hot Time in the Old Town Tonight" was a popular song at the end of the 19th century. One version of how it came about is that Theodore August Metz was traveling with the McIntyre and Heath Minstrels and when their train arrived at a place called Old Town, Metz could see through the window a group of children starting a fire near the tracks. One of the other minstrels said: "There'll be a hot time in the old town tonight," Metz noted the remark on a scrap of paper and incorporated it into the song he wrote the next day. Another version is that Metz first heard the tune played in 1893 at The Castle, Babe Connor's brothel in St. Louis, Missouri. Yet another is that Metz and his minstrels were in Hot Springs, South Dakota, where Joe Hayden worked at the Evans Hotel. He heard Hayden playing the song, which he said was from his youth in New Orleans and made it famous.

Hot springs are a natural phenomenon. They gush or trickle from the earth in hidden or unexpected places and their waters often contain beneficial minerals. Towns get their names from their proximity to one. In the United States, so many towns came to be called Hot Springs that the name eventually became nondescript. In March of 1950, the popular NBC radio TV quiz program Truth or Consequences hosted by Ralph Edwards, announced an essay contest: "Why does my town deserve a name change?" Edwards said the program would celebrate its tenth anniversary by broadcasting from the place where the contest winner lived. That turned out to be Hot Springs, New Mexico, a sleepy little village in the southern part of the state, which then changed its name to Truth or Consequences, T or C for short. For the next fifty years, Edwards visited the New Mexican locality each year and a series of festivities marked the date. The name change didn't do much for the place, though. Its population still hovers around 6,000. Its economy is still precarious. Its greatest attraction remains the series of hot springs offering rejuvenating soaks to visitors.

I have lived in the tropics, where heat is a constant. Because it is everywhere all the time, it is expected: an unalterable fact of life. People may exclaim *It's so hot*, but it's not as if anyone can imagine an alternative. Temperature and odor are cause and effect in such places. I can remember, during my years in Cuba, how sensitive people were to body odor; if they got the slightest whiff on a crowded city bus, other passengers would clear as wide a circle as possible around the presumed offender. Personal hygiene was at the forefront of every human interaction.

The first time I volunteered to cut sugarcane, I was in a barracks with fifty women and only three shower heads. The women lined up early in the morning before going out to the fields, then again before lunch and yet again at bedtime. I washed only in the evening and was called in by the camp director who suggested I might want to bathe more often like the rest of the women. Anything less was unacceptable. In the same period, the country's school uniforms included heavy gabardine jumpers for the girls and pants for the boys. Gabardine is a heat-retaining fabric, totally inappropriate at such latitudes. In that case, an inauspicious sense of style seemed to take precedence over the heat.

The adjective is understood as having different meanings depending on the context. Finding yourself in *hot water* is analogous to being in trouble. A *hot debate or discussion* is animated, lively, or passionate. A *hot contest* is intense, ruthless, highly competitive. When used to describe a book, song, film, or festival, the word is synonymous with important, interesting, worthwhile. You rarely hear a poem or painting spoken of in that way. A *hot topic* also means relevant, of the moment. *Too hot to handle* may refer to a subject that is considered socially off limits, for example, politics or religion or how much money a person earns. *Hot food* usually means food that is highly spiced rather than that which burns your lips.

Heat, real or metaphorical, is a powerful but often unexpected descriptor.

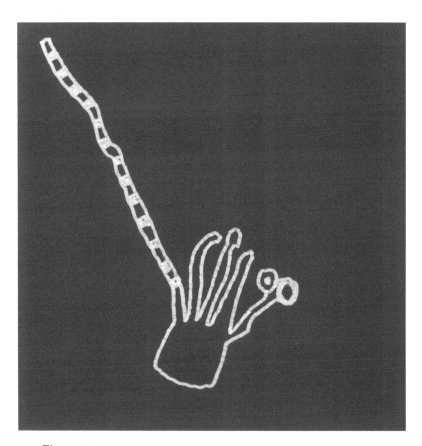

Figure 11

Adjectives

They're not what they seem.

While adjectives claim they modify or improve our understanding of a noun, that's not the whole story. They don't just show up of their own volition. We must look beyond their pretense at neutrality. Let me explain. If you see a mother out for a stroll with her two toddlers, one blond and blue-eyed, the other dark and sultry, and you exclaim over the first: *What a beautiful child*, then turn to the other and ask *Is this yours too,* you are saying the other child is ugly. Racism infuses the adjective. If you describe a variety of social systems and say only of capitalism that it *works*, you are telling us you believe the others don't. If you add *strong* or *able* to your description of one among several men, you are implying the others may be weak or inept.

Back when I was in school, we studied grammar by diagraming sentences. We were taught to place words on lines leading to further lines adorned with directional arrows and ranked by appearing above or below each other. The exercise was meant to teach us sentence structure and thus how to write and speak correctly. It always seemed absurd to me, one of those devices that illustrate the unimportant while ignoring what really matters. What really matters? The words themselves, their meanings implied as well as stated, the context in which they are used, and the tone of your voice.

For two years now, here in the United States we have lived with the word *steal* linked to the 2019 presidential election. *Stop the steal* was the phrase coined by that contest's loser as a way of getting the public to protest its outcome. This wasn't based on proof of any kind. And *steal* is a verb, not an adjective; it just plays the part of the latter in this situation. Words—even adjectives and adverbs—have a responsibility they may not be able to shoulder. *Fair* should be careful of the friends it chooses. Associating with *contest*, for example, in the moment may make it feel like one of the big boys, but history will surely judge it differently.

Very is one of those adjectives that runs around everywhere these days, attaching itself to any noun it can find. *How are you? Very well, thank you. Well* might suffice on its own but *very well* has become a figure of speech repeated until it tells us nothing. The responder may in fact be in a state anywhere between abject and excellent. *Fine* is another useless descriptor. We have gotten into the habit of saying we're *fine* even when we are anything but. Simple everyday words have lost their meanings with technology's strange bending of language.

Good is one of the least dependable adjectives in the language. We have corrupted it beyond recognition. *Be a good girl* usually means be the kind of girl society wants you to be, not the kind that meets your needs. *Be a good boy*, if the boy is white, means be entitled or opportunistic, regardless of whom you hurt. Be successful. If a boy is Black or Brown, *be good* may mean don't make waves, say sir, and keep your hands where the cop can see them. In recent years *bad* went rogue, tricking us by adding an extra *"a"* and passing itself off as its opposite. Adjectives like *hip, cool, dope,* or *woke* think a lot of themselves but don't realize they will have short lives.

Sometimes an adjective's devious nature can be spotted from miles away. If we know Jack hates Jim but refers to him as *That nice guy,* you can be sure sarcasm is involved and an ulterior motive is hiding in the modifier. *The respected Senator* is likely a tired courtesy, like *the honorable judge.*

And the woman with bruises on her arms and face who says her husband is *really a good person* is probably trying to convince herself as much as you.

Sometimes a different adjective linked to the same noun reflects the condition of the person speaking. A lobster thermidor referred to as *delicious, outrageous, expensive,* or *passable,* likely depends on the bank account of the person reporting.

You may believe you are on firm ground when it comes to talking about landscape. You'll get little pushback against descriptions such as *dramatic desert, mysterious forest,* or *calm or brutal sea.* Still, reality is in the eye of the beholder. Those who live in the desert, are familiar with the forest, or have spent their lives at sea, aren't as overcome by wonder as a visitor may be.

The thing to remember about adjectives, just as about adverbs and any other form of speech, is that the word itself is not responsible for its accuracy or how it may make you feel. A mouth utters the word. A mind is telling that mouth what to say. And informing that mind is either a spirit that is narrow and ugly or one that is bright, inclusive, and imaginative.

Fame

problematic subject, fame has a variety of meanings and evokes diverse emotions and sentiments. It is a shapeshifter among terms. We can generally agree that it implies being widely known, sometimes by millions or billions of people. It can apply to an individual, place, event, even an idea. Any of these may become famous, which is to say an important part of the culture, a reference. Or infamous—though the latter is more often referred to as notorious. *Rich and famous* is a one-stop destination, as if one condition were inseparable from the other. But that's not always the case.

For a person, fame may be deliberately sought and acquired with difficulty. Or it may be bestowed for reasons beyond the person's ambitions. It may come suddenly or slowly over a long period of time. It is usually accompanied by prizes and grants, the big ones that make it possible to live for several years at a time, often bestowed long after the recipient no longer needs the relief. It may bring surprise, arrogance, bafflement, or grace. The famous person may retreat into insularity or become a conscious mentor to others, giving back to younger generations.

What of the immense talents who died too young to be known? Or women whose gender rendered them invisible in their time? We are grateful for Mozart, who began composing at three years of age and lived long enough to give us some of the most beautiful music ever written. We feel outraged for Rosalind Franklin, whose x-ray diffraction studies provided crucial clues to the structure of DNA but was ignored when it came to the Nobel prize and died at the age of 37 from a cancer caused by her work in the lab.

And there are different kinds of fame. When I lived among artists in New York City, I knew some who acquired renown because they had an influential patron or hit on some gimmick that gained them instant popularity. Others, who were truly great, never made it beyond the confines of their own impoverished lives. They didn't know the right people, weren't willing to acquiesce to a passing fad, or didn't have a personality that encouraged recognition.

When fame comes during a person's lifetime, it alters that life in every way. When it comes posthumously, we lament its late arrival, saying: *If only she'd been a man* or *if we'd only known*. Fame is presumed a positive although that's not always the case. Early fame caused an artist I knew to repeat the same images over and over, confident they would sell and he would be able to conserve the lifestyle he'd attained. Once he'd gained the recognition that assured him that economic level, he stopped exploring. I always wondered how his art might have evolved had he favored his talent over security. But fame can also be a good thing, providing creative beings the space and freedom to explore their imaginations without having to worry about making ends meet at the day job they were encouraged to keep just in case. In an ideal social system this would not depend on fame but be simply the circumstance afforded all artists.

Our broken societies tend to exploit the glamorous individual rather than create mechanisms through which anyone may pursue their art. A lack of opportunity and censorship are enemies of creativity. Freedom to explore one's curiosity and move in unexpected directions is necessary to those in any field.

Fame invariably creates a distance: between those who possess it and their families and friends. That distance is a space that is likely to fill with complex emotions: jealousy, resentment, and other perverse feelings. Human interaction is affected. Relationships suffer. It can be ugly, occasionally dangerous. Time may bend to accommodate considerations that have little to do with who folks are or how they really feel. Most people are overly careful around the famous. They may be intimidated or are afraid to criticize or contradict them and hasten to do their bidding. They may also bask in the aura that surrounds them, hoping some of it will rub off.

Not infrequently those who have reached the pinnacle of success—in the arts, sports, science, politics, or any other arena—are different enough from the rest of us that they display visible signs of what we call mental illness. They may be labeled bipolar or schizophrenic. Ludwig van Beethoven, Michelangelo, Isaac Newton, Leo Tolstoy Vincent Van Gogh, Virginia Woolf, Vaslov Nijinsky, Sylvia Plath, and Robin Williams come to mind. We have long pondered whether excelling in a world of mediocrity drove these creators to affliction or if their unusual mental state was, in some way, a necessary component of their genius. If our societies were kinder and more tolerant of the unusual mind, would these people have been able to live less troubled lives?

Fame, when it comes, usually arrives with early maturity, and may diminish as the years pass. The aged dancer is no longer as limber as she was. The aged singer can no longer reach those high notes. The poet's voice has lost its power. The painter's colors have become muddy or flat. Sports stars past their prime can no longer pound the court or hit the balls or wrack up the points they once did. The scientific mind may genuinely explore in its youth, and age may induce it to focus more on the major prizes. A sage may be seen as richer in wisdom and therefore improved with age; but ours is a society that idealizes youth, and we are fickle when it comes to our heroes and heroines.

Variables such as class, gender and race can be ferocious obstacles to fame—even to simply excelling in one's chosen field. Marin Alsop had to face cruel pushback on her way to becoming the genius conductor she is today. Many believed a woman couldn't lead an orchestra. Had Alsop's talent not come to the attention of such as Leonard Bernstein, we might never have known her brilliance. Paul Robeson and Marian Anderson struggled against racism. The Williams sisters got the early tennis training they needed because their father was tenacious in bucking the class and racial barriers they faced.

We believe we know our idols, and our social attitudes about fame also make us believe we have the right to judge every detail of the famous person's life: if they should be condemned for extra-marital relationships, what sort of parents they are, whether they share our beliefs, even their diet and how they dress. Pound and Celine were fascists and inspired endless discussions as to whether that fact should influence how we read their poetry—or even if we should read it at all. Arguments can be made on both sides. On the one hand, we create from the essence of who we are, and our life philosophy naturally lives in what we produce. On the other, art is art. We should be able to appreciate it irrespective of its maker's ideology. Except in extreme cases, I tend to respond to the art independent of what I may think of its maker.

Fame can switch to infamy when we discover that the icon we admired plagiarized another's work, granted or withheld favors as a means of control, or sexually abused those over whom he or she exercised control. From one moment to the next, a person who enjoyed fame and all its privileges may find himself jobless, friendless, perhaps even facing prison for acts he considered his prerogative. This too, can cut both ways. During McCarthy's witch hunts of the 1950s, many talented individuals were prevented from working and rendered personas non grata because they were suspected of being Communists and/or refused to name others. Today's #MeToo movement has targeted famous men who have been forced to capitulate to the accusations of women no longer willing to accept their unwanted advances and power plays. These are not analogous examples. The mid-20th century harassment went against freedom of dissent and expression. Today's movement addresses behavior long encouraged in a misogynist culture that is finally being seen for what it is.

There are degrees of fame. You might be known in your neighborhood or community, a household name nationally or internationally, or someone as universally renown as Jesus of Nazareth, Joan of Arc, Shakespeare, Leonardo Di Vinci, Abraham Lincoln, Geronimo, Amelia Erhardt, Elizabeth Taylor, Che Guevara, Nelson Mandela, Pelé, or Serena Williams. The greater the fame, the less intimate the contact you have with your contemporaries; the familiarity between you and them decreases exponentially.

Fame is pursued and valued for all sorts of reasons. We must remind ourselves that it is a byproduct rather than a goal in and of itself. Hernán Cortés, Napoleon Bonaparte, Adolf Hitler, Pol Pot, Agosto Pinochet, Rodrigo Duterte, Jair Bolsonaro, and Donald Trump were all men who acquired fame through strongman tactics and criminal behavior. They left devastating legacies. By far more precious and deserved is the fame that comes from genuine brilliance and talent: that of Hypatia of Alexandria, Mahatma Gandhi, Charlie Chaplin, or Haydée Santamaría.

Fame is subordinate to what sparks it. And it's that which deserves our attention.

Smoke

Chameleon-like, to say the least, smoke can warn you of disaster, carry the scent of cedar on a winter night, or destroy your lungs. A graceful wisp may issue from a chimney, telling of a warm hearth within. Thick billows may choke you to death before you can reach the door. War photos showing towers of smoke invariably obscure the deaths of those unlucky enough to have been the target of a bombing or mortar attack. This season, like the last and the one before that, my horizon holds the residue of forest fires, smoke whipped by wind or layering upon the earth, clouding destination. *Where there's smoke there's fire* is our phrase of choice when we want to indicate that evidence invariably leads us to cause.

Atmospheric inversions trap dangerous air particles, often carrying the poisons of industry, and provoking havoc around the world. We have coined the word smog to describe the resultant mix of noxious smoke and atmospheric fog. The famous London fog of December 1952 trapped coal dust and other chemicals, killing an estimated 12,000 people. Because of its geological characteristics, Mexico City experiences such inversions every winter; the city has tried to resolve the problem by mandating that cars of a certain age with license plates ending in odd or even numbers circulate only on alternating days of the week. The Beijing Summer

Olympics of 2008 were threatened with cancelation because of extreme smog but the Chinese created an artificial climate, at least long enough to mitigate the immediate problem. Here in the United States, the air quality of Los Angeles and other densely populated cities has gotten worse over time. As industry flourishes and more cars and trucks use the highways, poisonous smog has become a deadly threat everywhere. It's as if civilization itself had a bad smoking habit.

And we individuals mirror our societies, reflecting their foibles, misplaced interests, dreams, and defeats. Looking back on my years of smoking, I see them as my personal version of a larger misadventure. We humans become mini representations of the world in which we live.

I started smoking cigarettes at fifteen, always out of my parents' sight. I would sneak one from the intricately adorned box always kept provisioned on the coffee table in our living room. Did it make me feel grown up, or was it simply teenage rebellion? My mother didn't smoke, and my father favored a pipe. Keeping cigarettes for guests was considered a courtesy back then. It expressed my family's upper middle-class aspirations. I remember that box with its overlay of copper, brass, and a white metal that may have been silver. Its design looked vaguely Middle Eastern. I saw it as an invitation.

By the time I was seventeen, I had a habit I couldn't break. Before I knew it, I was smoking three packs a day. Sixty cigarettes. I lit my first as I emerged from sleep, in half-darkness reaching for it on the night table and fumbling for a match. I smoked my last just before retiring for the night. Over the years, I progressed from Camels to Lucky Strikes and finally to one of those mentholated brands I hoped would soothe my raw throat and constant cough. It was called Salem; the package was my favorite blue-green and white. It made me think of the Salem witch trials, and I imagined a gesture of admiration for those misunderstood women. Certain people I knew smoked French Gauloises or Mexican Negritos. The fact that they regularly inhaled such strong tobacco imbued them with an aura of sophistication, a certain macho power.

By the time I was thirty, I coughed more than I was able to speak. My young son Gregory begged me to stop. He knew the burgeoning statistics and feared for my life. His concern for me then may have been the reason he never took up the habit.

My mother also tried hard to persuade me to give up smoking. She would clip articles from our hometown paper and send them to me to illustrate her position. But then, she also sent me articles that said coffee was bad for you, followed by others that claimed it was a newly discovered cure for cancer. Without her nagging insistence, I might have tried quitting earlier.

I was finally able to get rid of the habit two days after the birth of my youngest daughter, Ana. She was small—barely five pounds, perhaps a result of my smoking—and looked fragile when I brought her home from the tiny Mexico City clinic. I was sitting on my bed nursing her, a cigarette hanging from my lips, when I caught sight of our reflection in a full-length mirror across the room. The image that stared back showed a precarious wad of ash balanced above my baby's delicate head. Even the tenuous pulse of her fontanel might have dislodged it. The scene so disgusted me that I vowed to stop smoking then and there. I never picked up another cigarette.

Which is not to say that stopping was easy. On the contrary. A month after Ana's birth I was hit with a political repression that forced me underground, convinced my partner and me to send all four children ahead to Cuba, and began an extremely difficult and stress-filled period before we ourselves could escape Mexico. I still thought of cigarettes constantly, wanted one every waking moment. Not giving in was a form of resistance. I took it day by day. For almost a year my hands shook, and I would cry at the slightest provocation. But I held firm. And after a while I no longer had the habit. Even being near a smoker made me ill.

It's been more than half a century now. A diagnosis of emphysema is all that reminds me of the habit that once consumed me. Nicotine has not been my only vice, not even the most difficult. I had to battle overeating with equal determination and made many false starts. I was never a heavy drinker but stopped imbibing some four decades back and haven't had a drink since. I made that decision, among other reasons, because I have watched several good friends die from alcoholism. An addictive personality often has several outlets. And recovery can be a lonely road. My complete avoidance of hazardous substances feels good now: as if living free of them is an addiction, delicious in and of itself. Our corporate culture urges us to smoke, overeat, diet, drink, gamble, buy, and believe it's every lie, even as it warns us of the dangers inherent in all such activities. Mixed messages provide the soundtrack to our lives.

Like many old enough to do so, I can remember that panel of seven cigarette company executives raising their right hands before a congressional committee and swearing under oath they didn't know that nicotine was addictive. They were the first such men in suits and ties unable to get away with lying. It was 1994 and within two years all seven had lost their jobs. The nation's surgeon general at the time spearheaded an anti-smoking campaign that required warnings about cancer and death to be placed on all packs of cigarettes produced in the United States. Cigarette companies were also urged not to advertise to youth, a caution hard to enforce. Statistics show that eventually fewer people bought tobacco products. True to its colonialist nature, US companies intensified their sales of cigarettes to the dependent populations; if they couldn't continue to reap high profits among their own upper and middle classes, they would do so in ghettos, on Indian reservations and abroad. And then E-cigarettes came on the market. Rumor had it they contained less nicotine or were less addictive. Yet another trick. By that time, we knew that most corporate claims are lies: the acceptable language of commerce.

Those in power manipulate us into addiction. It guarantees reliable profit to those who just want to keep on selling, no matter what the human cost.

Exile

I was restless, curious. Striking out to see the world, my ten-month-old son in my arms, seemed the next logical step. It's sometimes been called self-imposed exile, but I never thought of it that way. I can't remember even thinking about whether or when I would return. One adventure at a time.

Forced exile is something else. I would experience this later, with all its fear and risk. You're in danger and manage to get away. We have many historic examples: the Old Testament's legend of the Israelites' retreat from Egypt, those Jews and others who managed to escape the European Holocaust at mid-20th century, Palestinians pushed from their homelands, thousands of Latin Americans who were able to evade disappearance, torture, and death during that continent's cruel dictatorships several decades later, refugees braving drowning in illegal crossings of the Mediterranean, and those today who flee authoritarian regimes throughout the world.

I began my forced exile in the fall of 1969. The year before, I had participated in the Mexican student movement and now suffered a repression that attacked me and my family from several insurmountable angles. The Cuban revolution had a policy of embracing people like us, and it immediately received my children, caring for them as it cared for so many others. A few months later, when I was finally able to get out of Mexico, Cuba took me and my partner in as well. I traveled to the Island via Czechoslovakia, the safest route at the time. My family and I lived in that Caribbean country for the next eleven years, participating in exuberant social change and reaping the benefits of a society rooted in social justice.

Exile is never simply leaving one place and arriving in another. It is a complete change of scene accompanied by profound anxiety. The new culture is different from anything experienced before. Most often, the exiled person must start over in confounding economic conditions. I knew many Latin American revolutionaries who were forced to remake their lives in countries where climate, politics, language, food, sense of humor, and many other aspects of life we tend to take for granted were so unfamiliar as to be unrecognizable. Doctors and engineers had to take jobs cleaning houses or caring for the dying.

I was fortunate that Cuba took me in. My family and I spoke Spanish, albeit a different Spanish than that which was spoken in our new home. And the culture, although unlike any we'd known previously, was new to the Cubans as well. They were working to create a society they hoped would be entirely different from the exploitative one they'd experienced in the past.

Still, these issues don't go to the heart of the matter. What part of my story could I reveal? What secrets must I keep? What of the friends, school and beloved teachers ripped from my children's lives? What of the new and complicated distance that suddenly stretched out between us and what had been our home? What of all the things we had to abandon in our hurried flight: not just physical place and opportunity but photo albums and other precious mementos? From the window of the taxi that took me from my last hideaway to the Mexico City airport, I watched neighborhoods and streets fade from sight. Would I ever see them again? Not knowing was its own anguish.

I tried to take solace in the stories of other exiles I knew about, multitudes or individuals. And I thought about those who tried to escape death-dealing scenarios but didn't succeed, people such as Walter Benjamin, who never crossed that last border during World War II, or the hundreds of thousands of refugees who every year die of exposure and thirst on the desert between Mexico and the United States. I was grateful for my privilege and connections. Yet the comparisons remained abstract. They didn't alleviate the emotional turmoil that being uprooted from place creates.

Gerda Lerner (1920–2013) was an Austrian-born refugee who came to the US escaping the Nazi takeover of her country. She was a brilliant feminist historian and someone I was proud to call my friend. I remember leaving Studs Terkel's radio recording studio in Chicago—this was sometime in the 1980s—just as Gerda was about to go in. She had been listening to my interview and offered a brief critique: *You did well*, she said, *but you didn't focus enough on the meaning of displacement. It's one of those things no one who hasn't experienced it can understand.* Since then, I have tried to explore exile in all its intertwined aspects: economic, physical, psychological, emotional, and in terms of cellular memory.

This attempt has led me to think about an even more devastating situation, that of those people who are born in bodies with which they don't identify. They are not forced to travel but their need for authenticity is with them constantly. Theirs is a problem of exile in reverse. Until recently, transgender people could contemplate no escape from the biological identities that imprisoned them. Now, although the route is often fraught with pain, a lack of social understanding, and ugly legal pushback, many may travel to a self they recognize.

Those belonging to races and ethnicities scorned by the societies in which they live have often chosen assimilation rather than opting for the pride of difference. My own parents, both of Jewish extraction, changed their surname and cut off from most of their relatives. They wanted to be accepted within the gentile mainstream. We have examples of African Americans who have chosen to pass as white, and even a few whites who have chosen to identify as African Americans because they were uncomfortable in their birth personae. Mass exhibitions of pride are a relatively recent phenomenon: Indigenous pride, Black pride, feminist pride, gay pride, trans pride, disability pride. For this pride to be accessible to most individuals and to impact society, it needs numbers: community.

Exile is a cruel weapon, whether forced by political mandate or adopted out of fear of what is to come. No one should have to live displaced, to escape their own identity, humanity, culture.

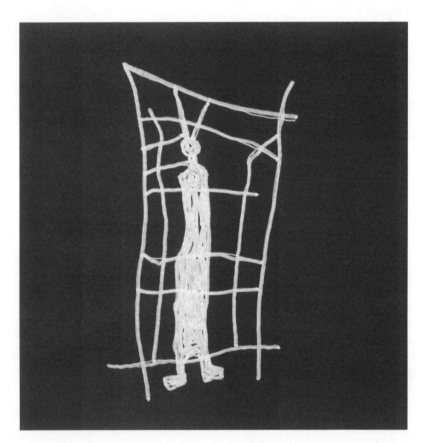

Figure 12

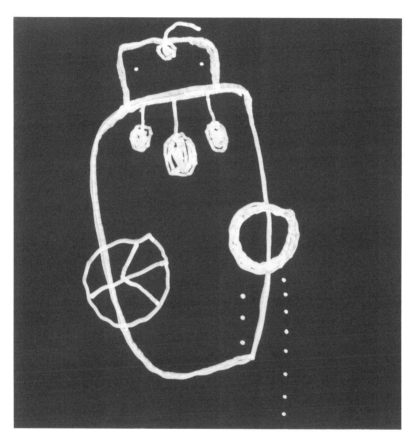

Figure 13

Quarantine

It's a household concept now. A virus called COVID-19 and its ongoing mutations have changed the way we live. As I write, the BA.5 subvariant, said to be the most contagious to date, invades lungs and, in a more complicated way, minds. People are newly afraid. Even those who have had all the shots and boosters and take all possible precautions fear what has come to be known as *long covid*, a form of the infection that lingers and can cause permanent organ damage. This is true all over the world, in all regions, among all races and cultures and ages, although the experience is profoundly different for those with economic means and those without.

More than two and a half years into the crisis, the aged and vulnerable continue to isolate. Contagion is on everyone's mind. We no longer hug or touch one another as we once did. Kisses, except among lovers and those in intimate pods, have become a thing of the past. Invisible droplets of saliva and even our breath itself have become dangerous. Will speaking kill the listener? Thousands are still sickening and dying every day. Despite this, some people risk going out again, seeing friends, running errands, and socializing in public places. As a poet who has spent the past two and a half years reading my work on Zoom, I am once again doing live events. We remain masked and cautious. The risk feels worth it.

There are important numbers of people who refuse to cooperate with the rest of the human community. They are unwilling to get vaccinated or take measures to protect themselves or those around them. Their motives vary. Some don't trust the vaccine. They may consider themselves invulnerable, and don't care enough about others. The most unreasonable are belligerent, insistent on demonstrating a bizarre individuality by refusing to engage in any practice that signals cooperation or generosity of spirit; yet when they fall ill almost always expect an overwhelmed health system to care for them. The polarization around COVID reflects a larger war in which lines have been drawn, opposing sides staked out, and unproductive decisions replace compassion and compromise. These days, proponents of both positions seem to be tired of explaining their actions; we all just charge ahead, frustrated and digging in our heels.

Three years ago, I couldn't have imagined writing a piece about quarantine. Today it's a mundane topic.

When people ask me if I am confounded by the way our lives have changed, I have two responses. On the one hand, I have known for a long time that a social unraveling would be the result of our disregard for where we live. You can't offend earth, air, and other natural resources so blatantly and continuously without expecting such an outcome. But that's the intellectual speaking. Emotionally, in terms of feelings that are more difficult to articulate, what has befallen us is shocking. Living the daily details is something for which we haven't been able to prepare. The current pandemic changed everything. We inhabit a new world.

I can't help wondering if this is how people felt during previous plagues. There were far fewer people on earth and greater distances between population centers. Immigrant ships and horses carried contagion more slowly than airplanes. We didn't have an internet that gave us immediate communication and instant access to information. But for those who lived then, the dangers surely must have felt as menacing.

The earliest recorded pandemic occurred in Athens during the Peloponnesian War in 430 BC. In 165 AD an early appearance of smallpox began with the Huns and then infected the Germans who passed it to the Romans. The Romans then spread it throughout their empire. Fifteen years later it claimed the life of Marcus Aurelius. The Cyprian plague of 250 AD reoccurred over the next three centuries, hitting Britain in 444 AD. The Justinian plague, 11th century leprosy, and the Black Death of 1350, all followed. Science was unable to offer today's solutions; chance and privilege alone determined life or death. Religion, on the other hand, increased its influence as the faithful attributed plagues to God's wrath and prayed to be saved. Individually, some of those same faithful acted selflessly and heroically to aid the victims; Mexico's illustrious poet nun Sor Juana Inés de la Cruz died from the plague she contracted while tending to her convent sisters in 1695.

What we now refer to as the Colombian Exchange—the host of fatal diseases brought by the Spanish with their conquest of the Americas—killed up to ninety percent of the original inhabitants north and south. In 1520 the Aztec Empire was almost entirely wiped out by a smallpox infection. Thus began the era in which disease was introduced as a colonialist weapon—first accidentally and then intentionally. Syphilis battered native peoples in South America. In what is now the United States, European Americans distributed small-pox-infected blankets to indigenous peoples with the unabashed intention of decimating their numbers and weakening their power. A succession of US administrations waged sterilization campaigns against women throughout the Americas, including Puerto Rico which is a part of our own nation. Although not a disease, this was also an effective way of reducing numbers of people they considered a threat.

In 1957 Asian Flu caused an estimated total of 1.1 million deaths globally. HIV/AIDS was first identified in 1981 and has so far killed 35 million people worldwide. SARS, Ebola and Zika followed. Some of these hit specific populations hardest: homosexual men or clusters in far-off African nations, allowing those who remained unaffected to bask in a false and bigoted sense of security that enabled them to evade responsibility.

COVID-19 is only the most recent pandemic to assault us. Although we know so much more about infection now, have developed vaccines in record time, and can distribute them quickly, inequality, political maneuvering, ignorance, and lies have so far produced more than a million deaths in the US and close to six and a half million globally.

These are statistics, numbers that often remain cold and distant in the face of our insularity. Our history has most often been written by observers rather than participants and has been recorded in ways that obliterate visceral memory. It emphasizes those qualities that make us proud and deemphasizes those that demand we engage in critical thought, learn from our failures, and reconfigure our assumptions, habits, and institutions.

There are times when disasters contradict each other, propelling people in seemingly contrary directions. Sweaty *raves* and newly denominated *cuddle parties* are the rage in Kyiv as bombing can be heard in the distance. Ukrainians suffer Russia's war and the virus simultaneously. Quarantine from both was the rule until the capital city's young people rebelled and actively pursued the human touch they'd so desperately missed for so long. The *cuddle parties* are especially noteworthy; participants seek out strangers and pull them close in non-sexual knots of bodies eager for human warmth. They say that these function as psychotherapy. Because of the curfew, the events begin mid-afternoon and end around nine or ten at night with the wail of the air-raid siren. The proceeds are often donated to the war effort and humanitarian relief.

In most of the world, we still observe some form of quarantine. Illness, death, individually calculated risk, booster shots, social distancing, masks, and frequent handwashing are here to stay. Despite the palpable damage, humanity will be required to adapt to this new normal as it does to other major life disruptions: global warming, continuous war, increased violence, endless human migrations, neo-fascist leaders, and those who support them. We may well be stuck with some form of quarantine for the duration. It's important that we avoid quarantining our minds and hearts, our capacity to work together for a more sustainable future.

Although we live with the physical constraints successive pandemics inflict, we must find ways to make people everywhere safer, healthier, less vulnerable. We must continue to love and create, think together, solve problems collectively, and promote the vibrant interaction that has brought us this far on our journey of making and doing.

In the Story

'd been writing these brief prose pieces for a while when my dear friend, the brilliant Suquamish poet Cedar Sigo, suffered a stroke. You don't expect that of someone in his forties, and I held the phone as if it had suddenly burst into flames. Cedar's voice was resonant as always, perhaps more careful, ponderous. *I had to learn to speak again*, he told me. *I'm still having trouble typing but I can read. Send me something to read.* We often exchange what we are working on and enjoy one another's feedback. And so, I sent two of these pieces off to him on those cyber wings that make communication, even from a distance, so immediate now.

My friend's initial feedback was *I can see that you are trying to remove yourself from the work.* It wasn't the response I expected but I could tell he meant it as a compliment. I was pleased but also mystified. Removing myself from what I write has long been a dilemma for me, a goal as well as an oxymoron. For as long as I've considered myself a writer, it's been an issue that's pulled me in one direction or the other. In another context, Cedar also said *I feel smarter now.* Later he amended that. *Perhaps more aware is a better way of putting it.* Life's fragility is a powerful teacher. I know near-death experiences can reorganize the way we see the world and our willingness to call things as we see them.

As a woman who came of age in the stifling 1950s, intentionally unmarried when I gave birth to the first of my four children and who had the next three with two different men, as a woman who discovered my lesbian identity at age fifty, as someone who—in short—was prone to breaking *the rules*, I often felt compelled to center myself in my story. It was my way of fighting invisibility. As someone who followed what seemed an obvious map to my belief that we must make the world better and safer, and that I have a role to play in that effort, I was in the story whether I wanted to be or not. As a creative being, I also put a lot of energy into making art that stands on its own, not dependent on a political message. Understand: not empty of political insight, just not always explicitly featuring it.

Over 87 years, I've learned again and again that I'm part of a community. More than one, in fact. And that those communities give me strength. I've wanted to situate myself in the places I've inhabited alongside all those who inhabit those places with me. Space and time. At war against the secrets and silences imposed upon us. Finding agency in witness and vulnerability.

In the 1970s, when I was doing oral history, I wanted my readers to experience my interviewee's stories free from my intervention. I remember struggling to remove the interviewer, myself, from those narratives. I experimented with different ways of doing that. The most obvious was to eliminate my questions, transcribing the story without interruption. Of course, I discovered that I was filtering the stories in many ways apart from simply including my voice. What questions was I asking? How was I asking them? What did I know about the lives I was presenting? Who held the power in those relationships?

Later, perhaps three decades ago, a friend arranged for me to meet his literary agent. He thought she might take me on, help me publish in this country in which literature is first and foremost a business. Over an awkward dinner, the woman suggested I write a memoir in which I drop the name of every famous person I'd ever met, however briefly. *Willem de Kooning. Hannah Arendt. Marilyn Monroe. Fidel Castro. You can blur the line between truth and fiction*, she said. I replied that I'd known Elaine de Kooning much better than her husband, that my relationship with Hannah Arendt had been superficial at best, that I'd spent a single afternoon with Marilyn, and that Fidel and I had only shaken hands and spoken a couple of times. If I wrote a memoir, it wouldn't be the one she had in mind.

Thirty years passed, and I did eventually write a story of my life. On my terms. My original title was *I Never Left Home: A Memoir of Time and Place*. That, I believed, would forefront my desire to emphasize the time I've lived and the places where I've done that living. I hoped it would steer readers to a journey not made in isolation but in the company of others. And convince them that those others were integral to my story. My editor, however, advocated for *I Never Left Home: Poet, Feminist, Revolutionary*. The publisher's promotional team felt it would help sell the book. I argued my preference but finally gave in. Didn't I, too, want as many readers as possible?

What does it mean to remove myself from my work, the most personal thing I create? Is such a thing even possible? Are we talking about absolutes, or matters of degree? A mirror gives back what it sees. Even if I avoid presenting myself at the center of my experience, I am writing out of that self, the accumulation of experiences that have taken me from there to here and what I have made of them.

I see with my eyes, hear with my ears, feel with this body that has been both abused and cherished. Paraphrasing the novelist Ann Quin, writing about visiting my 1960s home in Mexico City, I also might say I *hear with my eyes and see with my ears*. I am guided by the morality I have constructed, often through painful trial and error. The language in which I write uses words the way I have taught myself to use them: as accurately and creatively as possible saying what I mean. Inevitably, it is also a language that advertises my class, nationality, age, race, gender, sexual identity, mental and physical abilities, desire, taste, idiosyncrasies. Also, where I was born and grew up, in what sort of family, with what fears and possibilities.

Is it a good thing that my friend thinks I am removing myself from my work? An observation made from his newly honed ability to see beneath the surface. Is my shift, if it exists, a display of selflessness or exhaustion? Should I pat myself on the back or is it evidence, perhaps, of a world so frustratingly incomprehensible that it overwhelms the first-person singular?

Distraction

In conversation with Joan Macneil[14]

have come to believe that the most effective long-range weapon politicians and the corporate world wield against us is distraction. Toni Morison once observed that "The function, the very serious function, of racism, is distraction. It keeps you from doing your work. It keeps you explaining, over and over again, your reason for being."[15] If a long-cultivated system can distract, how much more immediately and easily can shortcuts like skillfully contrived crises, in-your-face advertising, and power-generated coercion do so. Morrison was speaking about the fear and hatred of those with dark skin, a crime that in the United States has its roots in slavery and our failure as a nation to deal with its cruel legacy. But her statement might apply as well to misogyny, homophobia, disdain for the poor or any othered group. And it applies to the way our news is reported, the emphasis or outright lies designed to keep us concerned with fake problems so that we won't think about the real ones.

---

14. Although I take responsibility for this text, it developed after I sent an early version to my friend Joan MacNeil, Canadian social activist and writer. I acknowledge her valuable critique and input.

15. In an address titled "A Humanist View" given at Portland State University in 1975.

Distraction has replaced persuasion in civic discourse. Extreme polarization prevents us from talking to one another.

We are so easily distracted today for two main reasons. In the first place, because activities such as watching television, playing video games, interacting with so-called automatic intelligence, and responding to advertising in all its subtle and unsubtle forms have largely replaced the slower, deeper, more contemplative activities such as reading or spending time alone or face to face with family and friends. And in the second, because we have become accustomed to, and in many ways dependent upon, an increasingly intense level of stimulation. Younger people especially seem to need this fever pitch: audio, visual, tactile. These changes have diminished our capacity for attention and made us easier targets for distraction.

Distraction can pass itself off as entertainment. It costs almost nothing and comes in every shape, color, and intensity of threat. Commercial and social media are its greatest allies. Newscasts, feature stories in magazines and newspapers, films, songs, serial television, pageants, internet postings, and all sorts of home screen specials have become almost indistinguishable from one another. They revel in anything from glitz to horror. Many emphasize gruesome crime, shocking violence, or a feel-good human-interest story that captures our attention in a way that the boring repetition of important information about global warming, immigration, or war cannot.

The New York Times has taken to adding the tag "5 min read" or "3 min read" below the headlines of its opinion pieces, as if assuring its subscribers that the text in question won't take up too much of our time. Even abbreviating *minutes* to *min* seems to be telling us: this won't take too long. The "newspaper of record" clearly feels it must compete with the instant morsels that flood today's digital communication: offerings too often high in wow value and notably deficient in the "who, what, when, where, and why" once so important in the practice of journalism.

Celebrity culture has become a constant distraction. And it's not just the occasional look at a fairy-tale life. We are urged to desire what the rich and famous possess and taught we can have a version of it by indebting ourselves forever or by working yet harder and longer. Healthcare, decent housing, healthy food, and other genuinely necessary items and services have become more and more difficult to come by, so the profiteers must distract us from believing we can remedy the lack or live perfectly well without. Then there are those constant pings and recorded calls on our cell phones that interrupt our concentration during the day, threaten our night-time sleep, and have become expected distractions. I can remember a "no call" service we used to be able to access to get on a list that blocked our telephone number from such annoyances; it no longer seems to function.

Slick advertising too often lures us with promises it knows are lies and keeps us from exploring solutions that can work. Will the latest fashion really make us happy? Is a diamond ring truly synonymous with love? Caught up in the manufactured drama created by the false claim of a stolen election or the miseries of a frustrated prince and his biracial wife, we don't think about the issues that most affect our lives and are destroying the life of the planet.

I want to make it clear that I'm not only talking about the rabid brand of Republican whose contempt for anything resembling ethics knows no bounds. Democrats too are guilty of using distraction as a tool to get what they want without too much thought as to what it means in terms of endangering the species and the environment. Distraction is commonplace. In fact, most institutions, or individuals with power over others, today make ample use of this weapon. In campaigning, in the exercise of political leadership itself, and in advertising and sales, the idea that the end justifies the means has become a constant at almost every level of interaction.

Distraction is an easy construct. It may be built on a famous person's urge to tell family secrets or a lie repeated often and with enough bravado that it is accepted as truth. For example, when not-yet-president Trump boasted that he could shoot someone dead on New York's Fifth Avenue and get away with it, rather than take the comment as the warning it was and turning against the bully, large numbers of people were titillated by it and voted him to the highest office of the land.

A single horrific scene of the destruction wrought by an out-of-control wildfire in California rivets us, while the hard facts of the climate crisis and the changes needed to address it seem too ponderous and complex to consider. Provoking public doubt about the science regarding COVID has also groomed segments of the public to be excessively skeptical about the scientific consensus regarding the causes of the climate crisis and the urgency of taking action to address it.

We have been conditioned to this distraction over a long period of time. For at least a generation, our public education system has been one of its most flagrant Petrie dishes. By emphasizing true or false testing over critical thinking, it trains our children not to reason for themselves but to chance answers that require no real thought and minimal effort. By removing music and the arts from school curriculums, it cheats those coming up of practices in which intuition and imagination play an important role and make the overall education experience less meaningful. In school districts where controversial subjects have been removed from textbooks and classroom discussion, students lose the opportunity to figure out what they think about the important questions of the day. Currently, a number of states have banned important books or removed them from school curriculums. Many children, especially those of poor families whose parents often have less formal education than the children's teachers, cannot develop their intelligence and talents, thereby acquiring the self-confidence needed to feel comfortable in life and learn to their full potential.

Religion also bears increased responsibility for distracting us. Superstitions, traditions, prejudices, rules, and prohibitions, set in centuries of stone, limit believers' ability to think for themselves. Fundamentalist megachurches and influential religious figures direct thousands to support retrograde political policies without giving thought to how those policies will affect their own lives. In the United Stated, ignoring our long-term separation of Church and State, we give a dangerous degree of power to religious institutions and the superstitions they engender.

Scandal's momentary excitement grabs us. We are lured by the astonishing or shocking. Our attention span is brief: we tire of any story quickly and are soon caught up in the next dramatic tale. This can be seen in the ways in which instant internet communication has left thoughtful discourse behind. Emoticons have taken the place of a sentence or two of our own creation. Self-expression has been reduced to readymade memes, rendering the exploration of creativity and language a thing of the past. Many people, although desperate for transformational change, have been lulled into thinking that "liking" a Facebook post is the same as organizing, and they never get on with the communal work of actually engaging in concrete political action.

It may be argued that the internet has brought us together, linked people all over, equalizing social classes and making research easier and the global village smaller and more accessible. This is true. But there are two sides to every story. With such easy access to studies about health, climate, the economy, or any other urgent issue, and with the immediate availability of so many goods and services, how do we separate the information put out there by companies selling a product from that produced by serious scientists or economists undertaking investigations not beholden to big money? Corporate lies are routine, and whistle-blowers no longer considered heroes. How do we know whom to trust? Social media magnify these problems, stoking anxiety and making us easier prey for conspiracy theories and other simplistic (non)solutions.

Indeed, trust has become a rare commodity in contemporary US life, and not one that is particularly valued. In the 2022 midterms, a hard right Republican named George Santos was elected to the United States House of Representatives. His entire curriculum vitae was a lie, from a non-existent university degree to his employment history and even his ethnic origin. He said he was Jewish, later claiming that he meant Jew-*ish* when the lie was discovered. He even claimed that his mother had been in the New York Trade Center's south tower on 9/11, although she wasn't even in the country at the time. Santos uses fashion to distract those who question his authenticity: the button-up white shirt, crew-neck sweater in the old-school colors of periwinkle and gray, blue blazer and khaki trousers which are the uniform of preppy private-school boys and do such a good job of fooling his constituents. Despite a few mild criticisms from other congresspeople who think they should echo the outrage sparked by his deceit, he took his place in the governing body. He has finally been legally charged for some of his crimes but remains in Congress pending the case's outcome. Lies on the part of our politicians no longer bring them down.

We have been distracted from thinking for ourselves and from thoughtful discussion with others. We are so used to taking the quick and easy path to personal conviction, the longer, more trustworthy path seems old-fashioned, time-consuming, and outdated. We no longer know who is trying to inform us and who simply wants to make a profit from our needs, both fabricated and genuine. Ever larger and more mesmerizing television screens seduce us with images of material goods we feel will solve our every problem, and so-called truths that seem to make sense in a context of immediate gratification and extreme polarization.

Political participation is often reduced to deceitful distraction. For example, we receive an invitation to sign a "birthday card" for a public figure we admire. What a nice idea, we may think. But the invitation invariably leads to a plea for money. Or the telephone rings and someone asks if we will take a brief survey; it will only take a few minutes of your time, the voice assures us. If we consent, the survey may end with that familiar appeal for a donation. Or we may not notice that the survey's questions are rigged to produce certain answers. If we complain, we often find ourselves doing so to a recording that cannot hear us. All these are forms of manipulation that distract us from meaningful communication and the transmission of honest information.

Those of us with a certain level of intellectual or political sophistication may think we aren't duped by such deceit. I don't believe any of us are immune. The very insistence with which we are bombarded by these distractions traps us in a web we may have trouble identifying, much less be able to ignore.

In the United States we are anaesthetized by the idea that we are the best, most advanced, at the forefront of knowledge and invention. It may surprise many people to learn this isn't so. Numerous countries equal or outrank us in knowledge, invention, innovation, education, wellbeing, and in taking responsibility for meeting their citizens' needs.

How, you might ask, can we escape distraction? Where do we find legitimate research, dependable information? It is important to try to free ourselves from bias, to listen to all voices. The sources are there, often hiding in plain sight. One question we should ask is: what institution produced a study or report? Whose interests does it serve? We must resist being taken in by phrases such as "the experts say." What experts and what are their qualifications? We mustn't be intimidated by fancy titles or the money that backs vast campaigns. Learn to ask questions.

Today many artists—poets, writers, musicians, painters, photographers, and other visual artists—are producing work that centers our attention on the widespread distraction that has been weaponized against us. I don't believe it is art's purpose to do this. But when it does, it can be a very powerful call to attention.

Distraction is an invisible bullet that maims and can even kill before we see it coming. In fact, we may never see it coming, so expertly have we been conditioned to ignore its insidious aim, and so distracted are we by the tsunami of useless attention-grabbing information bombarding us day after day. The alternative is for each of us to resist, pay attention, reconnect with our questioning nature, and refuse to participate in our own ignorance and demise. It's not easy for us as individuals to struggle against powerful corporate or political interests. But, together, it is possible. Small victories can lead to larger ones. There is surprising strength in recognizing manipulation, taking action, and joining with others to reject what deceives and harms.

28 Flavors

When I was a child, family road trips often included a stop at a Howard Johnson's. You might spot the orange roof, signature cupola and weathervane, and the aqua and white exterior colors of the restaurant in any city or town. I know that at least 1,000 existed throughout the country at the height of its popularity. HoJo's, as we called the chain, was especially famous for its 28 flavors of ice cream. You could ask any waitress what they were, and she would recite alphabetically from memory:

Banana
Black Raspberry
Burgundy Cherry
Butter Pecan
Buttercrunch
Butterscotch
Caramel Fudge
Chocolate
Chocolate Chip

Coconut
Coffee
Frozen Pudding
Fruit Salad
Fudge Ripple
Lemon Stick
Macaroon
Maple Walnut
Mocha Chip
Orang-Pineapple
Peach
Peanut Brittle
Peppermint Stick
Pineapple
Pistachio
Strawberry
Strawberry Ripple
Vanilla

If, halfway through, you interrupted the aqua-aproned young woman with: *Wait, I didn't get that last one, can you go back?* she would have to start over. Rote memorization of the list was a requirement of her job. As children, my brother, sister, and I would stop the litany just to make her repeat the entire list. And we'd giggle mercilessly. It was one of those mean tricks that children learn to play on adults.

It occurs to me that reciting those 28 flavors was a performative version of Andy Warhol's Campbell Soup cans or Jasper Johns' American Flags: a piece of Americana of a particular era when the postwar message was *land of plenty,* and certain artists were challenging that message in their work. The country was charging full speed ahead in its creation of a commodity culture, blinding us to the fact that growing numbers of citizens were forced to consume the chemical deception of canned goods, the flag symbolized a patriotism distorted at its root, and the variety implicit in more than two dozen flavors of ice cream could only be enjoyed by those with the economic means to choose—the rich and that vast strata of US Americans who took to calling ourselves *middle class*. The corporation performed its message unconsciously. The artists were brilliantly cognizant of what they were creating.

Howard Deering Johnson started Howard Johnson's in Quincy, Massachusetts in 1925. It began as a pharmacy. When he discovered that its most popular feature was its soda fountain, he began expanding the sale of ice cream products. Howard Johnson's fortune rose and fell with the market crash of 1929 and subsequent economic ups and downs. What started out as a family enterprise eventually became one of the first national and international franchises, the most popular restaurant in America.

Although Howard Johnson's establishments were often both hotels and restaurants, the soda fountain was always the main attraction. And like so many soda fountains, its version followed a brutal path to desegregation. In the 1950s and early '60s, the Congress of Racial Equality (CORE) organized protests and sit-ins at Howard Johnson's locations throughout the south. In 1957, a Howard Johnson's in Dover, Delaware refused service to Komla Agbeli Gbedemah, the finance minister of Ghana, prompting a public apology from President Eisenhower. In the 1960s, the chain was known as gay-friendly, especially in New York City, and the Mattachine Society encouraged its patronage.

McDonalds with its golden arches has invaded every country on earth. It even has outlets in Mongolia and Bhutan. When the United States is at a political standoff with a nation, the name of the franchise might change to reflect a native identity, but the food remains basically the same. Like so many other once-popular brands, Howard Johnson's eventually faded from the landscape. It didn't have the staying power, probably because McDonalds and other more successful brands had better marketing. Today, you might see an updated version of the orange and aqua edifice here or there, but it's no longer a ubiquitous landmark. It remains in my memory, example of a time when look-alike and act-alike fast-food dispensaries were beginning to define a national culture, taking attention away from those many which are authentic to a locale.

Names

The first mark of a person's unique identity is their name. Their first name. In every culture, parents endow their children with names that embody ritualistic beliefs, carry a hope for the child's future, renew the memory of a dead relative or denote the lineage of one who is still alive. Jewish tradition, eminently patriarchal, gives boys a male family member's name. Ashkenazi Jews favor the name of the paternal grandfather, if deceased; Sephardic Jews may use that of a living relative, often the boy's father. Jewish girls are given Old Testament names.

Traditional Chinese girl's names include what in English would translate as Fragrance, Swallow, and Willow, evoking natural grace and beauty. Throughout Christianized Latin America, millions of girls are named María, the boys Jesús. For the same reason, Mohammed is a popular name among Muslim boys, while the native language translations of the more lyrical Smile and Bringer of Happiness are common for girls. Native Americans who follow tribal custom give their children names that express a characteristic. Ahanu (he laughs) is a popular Algonquin name, Ahiga (he fights) is popular among the Diné, and Ahote (restless one) among the Hopi. City or acculturated Indians sometimes choose names that astonish. I knew of a family in which three brothers were Harrison, Garrison, and Harley Davidson.

During the 1970s, when I lived in Cuba, many of the country's women had names like Milady, Dulce (Spanish for sweet), and Usnavy (the parents of the latter had seen the letters on the underside of a US military plane). Xiomara (ready for battle) and Valeria (strong and brave) soon became popular. As the Cuban revolution turned toward the Soviet Union, boys were named Vladimir, or sometimes Bladimir—the B often used in place of the V in the Island's rural version of Spanish. A young girl on our block was Krupskaya, after Lenin's wife. As the country began receiving the refugee children of revolutionaries throughout the Continent, those with the names of Russian, Chinese, and other heroes arrived. I remember four little Panamanian brothers called Stalin, Mao, Lenin, and Che. Even in that heyday of revolutionary fervor, we pitied the oldest. At the same time, hippie couples in the United States were choosing names such as Sky, River, Cloud, Dawn, and Meadow for their children.

In countries with strong indigenous roots, such as Mexico, girls are often called Citlali, Xochitl, or Nahuí, names descended from Nahuatl. The weight of conquest is strong, though, and most Mexican girls are called María in conjunction with another female name: María Cristina, María Elena, María Rosa, María del Carmen.

I don't come from a family of strong religious or cultural traditions, so when it came time for me to name my four children, I drew on more personal references. My firstborn was a boy. I named him Gregory. Friends asked if I had Gregory Corso in mind, or Gregory Peck. I explained that I'd been thinking of the Gregorian calendar and that I simply like the name. My next child was a daughter. Long before her birth, I knew I would name her Sarah; the biblical story of Sarah at the well had made an impression on me at the Quaker Sunday School I'd briefly attended when young. But by that time, I was married, and my husband argued for Dhyana, with its Buddhist and yogic roots. Our daughter became Sarah Dhyana. Today she teaches Kundalini Yoga, and I can't help wondering if her name led her to that practice.

My third child was another girl. During my pregnancy I'd been reading *El Mío Cid*. I named my little girl Ximena after the hero's wife. This was a popular girl's name in Spanish, but in most countries it was spelled with a J rather than an X. The X may have been a nod to Mexico's pre-Columbian cultures. By the time my youngest, another girl, came along, I no longer needed literary references or those from other cultures to help me name my offspring. I immediately knew that I wanted to call her Anna. As soon as she was old enough to make her own decisions, she dropped one of the N's, simplifying the spelling to Ana, more common throughout the Spanish-speaking world.

I am Margaret, and in my case there's a curious story connected with the name. My mother gave birth to another girl before me, who died shortly after she arrived. She'd been Margaret as well. I often wondered why I'd been given a name that already belonged to someone else, even if no longer alive. My mother clearly loved the name, though, and in my parents' relationship, she got what she wanted. My father had chosen Phyllis. Margaret feels right to me, and I've never had the urge to change it to some new age or esoteric designation. As a child and young girl, I was called Meg, after the oldest sister in *Little Women*. A few friends who knew me back then continue to call me by that name. During my many years in Latin America, few referred to me as Margarita. Often, though, Latin Americans spell my name *Margareth*. The added H always annoys me. I have no idea why.

My wife is Barbara, common in her parents' generation when it came to naming girls. When people call her Barb, it rubs her the wrong way. And when they call her Barbie, well, you don't want to know. Over the many years of our relationship, like most couples we've created names of endearment for one another. *Beezle. Megilee. Tree. Bear. Little Squirrel of the West by Southwest. Timburlache.* It's a constantly evolving list. All these endearments have their roots in shared experiences or intimate stories. They feel good on the tongue.

Last names also carry meaning. They can endorse or betray. In the late 19th and early 20th centuries, officials at the Ellis Island port of entry to the United States often misunderstood a European emigree's surname and recorded it wrong, changing it from then on. The refugees themselves sometimes shortened their old-country names, believing a more streamlined version would help them assimilate. Prejudice against, and a desire to distance oneself from one's ethnicity, may entice a person to change their last name. The Jewish Holocaust drove many to adopt gentile surnames. I wonder if some Muslims, who face such cruel abuse today, may take the same route.

There is power in a name, whether given by one's parents or oneself. We make peace with, live up to, or try to do proud what we are called. Which is why the slurs aimed at us by bullies and the numbers assigned us by prisons or concentration camps are meant to dehumanize and destroy the individuality a unique name bestows.

Refusing to answer to such insult, demanding to be called by the name of our choice, is important. It is an act of pride, often also of resistance.

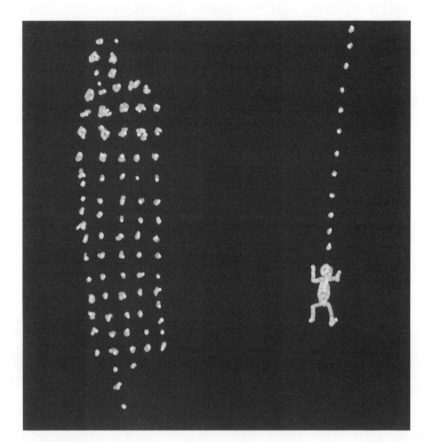

Figure 14

Figure 15

Luck 1

Is it fortuitous, or do we work for it? What do good and bad luck really mean? Luck is passive, something that happens to a person rather than that person doing anything to earn or provoke it. Not everyone would agree. When considering those who have lost their jobs, are living on the street, and face dubious futures, some say: *bad luck*. They don't consider the economy's drastic downturn, mental illness, or what may have induced the person in question to get hooked on drugs. A horrible childhood, vicious war, or other trauma aren't part of the equation. *It was just bad luck*, they say.

And bad luck is often misread. When a person is diagnosed with cancer or some other serious illness, people often ask if they were smokers or drinkers or in some other way imply that they are to blame for their illness which is just bad luck.

When hoping for success, the gambler will call on *Lady Luck*. She is the mythical figure no one really knows but who may casually appear with come-hither eyes, a low-cut gown, the pale scent of expensive perfume, and a cigarette held between heart-shaped lips. He may bribe her to stay at his side. If he wins, he believes she has touched him with her magic wand. If he loses, he will curse her.

Can we ascribe the hellish death of millions to something as ephemeral as luck? The Nazi mass murder of European Jews had its roots in the most egregious anti-Semitism. Pol Pot's extermination of a fourth of Cambodia's population showed that a crazed left as well as a degenerate right could sink to history's depths. Most wars record atrocities committed by both sides. Luck has nothing to do with these scenarios. They are born of pure hatred and a failure to combat that hatred before it causes incalculable harm.

In the mid-sixties, I agreed to ferry a guerrilla commander across the Guatemalan border into southern Mexico. I was a naïve young US American woman, filled with guilt for the crimes my government was committing throughout the world. I wanted to help. We crossed the border in my shiny Toyota, but suddenly found ourselves stopped at an immigration post we hadn't expected. The commander, a slight dark man with Indian features, got out of the car to speak with the officials. I sat frozen at the wheel, crossing and uncrossing my fingers and praying for *luck*. What might that luck look like? I had no idea. I only wanted us to be safely on our way.

We were *lucky* that day. It had more to do with the stupidity of those who briefly had us in their sites than it did with anything we ourselves conjured. My passenger, who had no papers, might have been imprisoned or deported. I would certainly have been charged with aiding a fugitive. Our story had a different, better, ending. Was it *luck* or some mix of ingenuity and chance?

Years later I faced another government in very different circumstances. I had lost my US citizenship and was trying to regain it by returning to the country of my birth and applying for residency with the intention of requesting reinstatement of nationality when the requisite time elapsed. By then, I had authored many books, several of which expressed strong disagreement with US policy in Southeast Asia and Central America. The US Immigration and Nationality Service ordered me deported based on my writing. I had a great legal team, widespread support, and the strength to see the struggle through. Would I have to leave my homeland, or would I be *lucky* and win the case?

I did eventually win. My citizenship was restored, and I've been able to live out my later years surrounded by family, the familiarity of culture and language, a humor I understand, and a landscape I love. Can I ascribe my win to our creativity and persistence? The skill of my lawyers? The political tenor of the times? A court that favored me, three to two? To all the above or to *luck*? At any point along that journey a motion or proceeding could have gone in the opposite direction. Who can say what combination of factors facilitated the outcome?

Some say luck, like love, is in the eye of the beholder. What pleases one invariably upsets another. Historically, it's often seemed like some perfect storm of elements pointing in the direction that shaped the outcome. *Dumb luck* has been used to describe the second law of thermodynamics, which posits that things fall apart. But I say that if they fall apart, they also come together. Randomness is central to my belief system.

What I know is that today we need much more than *luck*, however that is defined. We need decision and determination to cool an overheated world, stop wanton violence in its tracks, cultivate respect as necessary to the perpetuation of life, and honor peace in all its forms.

Luck 2

n times of trouble or catastrophe, those who are unaffected often express some version of the phrase: *How lucky I am!* Untouched by the calamity, they ascribe their salvation to that mysterious element we call luck. Luck's default position is good, although bad luck is just as arbitrary. And good and bad luck can intertwine in complex ways. A dear friend, describing life with her partner who suffers from incipient dementia, recently confided: *We have a rich and lovely relationship, and we are both drowning.*

The concept of luck is devoid of effort and responsibility. It just happens. And we like to pretend that it's random, although when we scratch the surface it's immediately apparent that economic status, connections, mobility, nationality, age, health, race, gender, sexual identity, willingness to conform to cultural expectations, and other variables all conspire to determine how lucky or unlucky we are. Good luck and privilege are not synonymous although they often go hand in hand. And we don't get lucky by exploiting or cheating others. Then we are opportunists or criminals.

I escaped detention, was able to take refuge in an embassy, and was lucky enough to be granted asylum in France. That was a statement made by a Chilean revolutionary friend following Pinochet's 1973 coup. She found luck in a horrific situation. *I'm lucky not to be experiencing terrible side effects and the treatments seem to be working,* said my friend diagnosed with stage-four esophageal cancer. He had accepted the fact that he had the disease and now considered himself lucky or unlucky within its confines. After the shock of terror or misfortune recedes, luck is perceived in a more circumscribed way.

We are often misled by what we consider the luck of others. In high school I idolized one of my classmates. She was beautiful and popular. It was no surprise that she was voted cheerleader and homecoming queen. I yearned to be her. Years later I heard that she had become a miserable alcoholic. She died young. When I discovered that even in her seemingly perfect youth she'd suffered from her father's abuse and society's impossible expectations, that her high school success had been a façade hiding painful secrets of shame, I had to revisit how I'd perceived luck.

The COVID-19 pandemic exercises our understanding of luck in new ways. We may consider ourselves lucky if we haven't been infected or if we've experienced the virus only briefly and without residual damage. We may not spend much time considering what we did to achieve the outcome, whether we were vaccinated, observed social distancing, wore a mask, or washed our hands every chance we got. It's often easier to ascribe our escape from misfortune to luck than to analyze factors that aren't easily quantifiable, and so difficult to consider as cause and effect.

We rarely use the word luck to describe success when talking about acts fraught with social stigma. To succeed at suicide, for example, may not be regarded by most people as lucky.

A biopic about one of my era's most iconic film stars, put forth the idea that luck is an art form. *You create your luck,* said Paul Newman. Six episodes followed him through acting school into dozens of successful roles. He and his second wife, Joanne Woodward, managed one of the longest relationships in a culture of short-lived marriages, and had several beautiful children. He was also shown to be a person of impressive ethics, who dedicated his fortune to projects which, long after his death, continue to aid terminally ill children and others in need. The feature's emphasis was on how hard he worked to achieve his goals. Luck, for him, was indeed an art form. Yet not entirely. At one point we hear him say: *I was born white, male, and with blue eyes.* Obvious elements of advantage.

When I consider my own life, I would say that I do believe in luck as an art form—although that's only one of its characteristics. I work at it every day, with that same mix of talent and discipline with which I embrace my writing. I am also profoundly grateful for certain conditions I didn't choose. I know how fortunate I am to have been born in a country not at war on home terrain and into a family that loved and nurtured me. I feel immensely lucky to be female at a time when girls grew up subjected to absurd restrictions—I still hold the cellular memory of that confinement—and then to have grown into womanhood at a time of powerful rebellion. Even back when people tended to remark of good poets: *She writes like a man,* I never wished to be one.

I am lucky to have had loving parents who did their best to give me opportunities, and more than a few mentors who taught me generously. Many dear friends are gems in my life. I am lucky to have inhabited places that have given me the wonder of landscape and two strong legs that enabled me to access some of its secrets. I am lucky to have asked questions and followed my intuition into struggles that have made me proud. To have participated in sociopolitical experiments designed to improve the ways in which we live together, even when so many of them failed to meet our expectations—or failed entirely.

I am immensely lucky to have given birth to four extraordinary human beings who, in turn, have given me ten grandchildren and three great grandchildren so far. I am lucky to be someone who has taken risks, values justice, and had the courage to fight for what I believe. Lucky to have been able to extradite myself from bad relationships and then enter a union many didn't understand at first, that has so far brought me 37 years of joy. I am lucky to have overcome a recent bout of Sepsis, a touch and go experience from which I wasn't sure I would emerge. I am lucky to be alive and relatively healthy at 87, having witnessed unspeakable tragedies and glimpsed elusive solutions. Possessed of such luck that their composite feels visceral, a living breathing companion.

I believe some of my luck can be traced to chance, factors beyond my making or control. I also know that I have enhanced that luck through intuition, courage, and hard work. Luck, for me, is a fabric of many colors, woven by many hands. Access is, at least in part, knowing when to reach out and hold on.

War

N **o.**

Hell no, we won't go! Hundreds of thousands chanting that promise in unison still sound in my ears from my youth, a time when massive protest got results.

That's all I really want to say about that, to quote the endearing fictional Forest Gump and my own conscience. But inveterate wordsmith, I can always be counted on to say more. Perhaps less really is more on such a topic as this. Still, I find myself continuing to unpack my arguments, explain my case.

There is rarely an excuse for war. I only consider fighting in self-defense to be acceptable. Every war ever fought has left its legacy of death, displacement, sorrow, and destruction. Spouses forever widowed. Children bereft of their parents. Parents without sons and daughters. Death beyond our ability to imagine. And the loss of irreplaceable landscape and cultural treasure.

Those who don't die may sustain injuries that cripple them for life. And the trauma of shellshock is the inevitable prelude to a different kind of death: PTSD, depression, homelessness, uncontrollable violence, homicide, suicide, and expressions of rage and despair that lead to further loss of life.

Many of our mass shooters are veterans whose war wounds were ignored by a society that shows its gratitude by repeating: *Thank you for your service*, and then abandons those veterans to fend for themselves.

Cities can be rebuilt, and the lost treasure replaced. Reconstruction earns billions for industries that favor war and mercenaries eager to fight anywhere they are well paid. It multiplies their profit, and we too can make money, investing in the war industry and in post-war reconstruction. There's more than enough profit to go around.

The loss of human life is final. A perverse sense of patriotism is fostered to make people believe they must sacrifice themselves to *keep their country safe*, when simple reason tells us there's is no danger to them and theirs. They are taught to fight and kill others who hold the same desires and dreams. These soldiers don't know their enemy. In most cases their own government's propaganda machine has told them just enough to make them believe he will get them if they don't get him first.

And the difference between enemy combatants and collateral damage is ever more blurred. In wars of old, soldiers marched out to meet their adversaries on well-defined battlefields. They were dressed in brilliant regalia and confronted soldiers decked out as they were. They charged with flags unfurled, to the sound of trumpets blaring. Then planes were invented and bombing raids could demolish whole cities from the air. Now technicians halfway around the world sit before computer screens and aim remote crosshairs at tiny specks that don't resemble anything human. Beyond the brilliant technology this represents, it was thought the distance would enable fighting men and women to kill more easily in a more abstract context. Not so. We now know those killing from afar are just as likely to suffer the post-traumatic stress of those who watch napalm consume a hut with a family screaming inside or are forced to thrust a bayonet into living flesh.

Modern warfare can poison the earth for generations. I walked what had once been fertile fields south of Vietnam's 17th parallel and didn't see a blade of grass. The earth was barren, unyielding; it looked like plastic. We can drop bombs like our nuclear 9,700-pound *Little Boy* over cities, vaporizing every living thing within its radius of death, and we did so at Hiroshima and Nagasaki. Such blasts can and frequently do put an end to a children's playground, a hospital ward, a birthday party, or wedding. Land mines continue to maim and kill, while the genetic mutations from Agent Orange and other chemicals do damage generations into the future. Those making war today kill indiscriminately and, if necessary, apologize later. The phrase of choice is *we regret*.

I can still remember the wars of my childhood and youth, those global conflagrations that promised to put an end to war: World War II, Vietnam. Just as our leaders tried to convince us that one final overwhelming attack saved lives because it produced the enemy's surrender, the horror of holocausts and genocides projected images that claimed they would bring lasting peace. Millions have been murdered simply as a show of force. Each of the lies betrayed every bombastic pledge, every anguished listener. The narratives death camp survivors tell and the photographs of skeletal bodies from which we turn away in horror live on in books and films: would-be deterrents become entertainment.

I have also known guerrilla wars, fought selflessly for emancipation and freedom. I supported them, especially when all peaceful efforts toward social change had been exhausted. I still believe those wars were justified, exceptions to the rule. But history has shown me that societies created through military campaigns inevitably contain the seeds of militarization that get in the way of bottom-up government. The future is always present in the means employed to reach a goal.

In our so-called democracy, when the public or our rule of law demand justifications for going to war, those justifications are easily fabricated. *Weapons of mass destruction. Irrefutable proof.* Once the planes with their cargo of death are airborne, nothing can stop them. And once our fighting men and women are on the ground, we say: *Well, we've got to finish what we started.*

We always hope voters will tire of war and choose leaders who promise not to make it. Many of us do tire of the repeated horror. But candidates lie about their intentions. Remember Nixon's promise to end our war in Vietnam and Johnson's pledge not to bomb Cambodia? Even in that rare instance when Congress refuses to authorize the invasion of a sovereign nation, those intent on attacking find undercover ways to channel funds, weapons, mercenaries. *Iran Contra* was one example of this, Iraq another.

Today wars succeed wars with neither explanation, discussion, nor approval. Governmental geopolitical considerations are all that matter. We may send our own people to die or provide the war materiel and expertise to surrogates. The bottom line is that war is here to stay, and our technological advances make it increasingly devastating.

When I try to understand why this is so, I am often told that aggression has been bred into us from the beginning of time. This explanation holds that humans had to fight for what we needed or die of hunger and cold. Without violence and war there would be no survival. That this innate characteristic has accompanied our development and cannot be excised. This may contain an element of truth, but I don't believe we can't change. Surely, we should be capable of redirecting our ethical compass, especially if it's so clearly to the planet's advantage.

We have always sought what we consider to be progress, even when some progress clearly contradicts the health of our planet. We perpetuate the production of fossil fuels, even when we know they are our downfall. We have lived by old rules and then been capable of changing them, becoming ever more inclusive and respectful of others. We make war after war, and here too we have a choice: radically change the way we solve our differences or annihilate humanity and all the beauty it has created.

If I believed in original sin, war would be that sin. I don't believe these are difficult choices. But as I write I know that these words of mine—and all the words uttered by anyone who has ever advocated against violence— echo uselessly in ears that refuse to listen.

These pages are not going to put an end to war. But I wouldn't be me if I didn't write them.

Voices

I am walking a disappearing trail on Jordan's Wadi Rum, multicolored dunes rising on all sides: red, purple, orange, streaks of pale green, creamy brown. Although I have come a mere mile from camp, I have the sense I am alone on earth—so absent of other humans is the landscape that stretches before me. I wonder if what I hear is a soft breeze making distant ripples in the sand. Even when I cannot decipher them, I could swear those are words. Arabic is one of the world's 7,137 languages I don't know.

At the mouth of a shallow alcove in northern Arizona called Massacre Cave, the high-pitched sound of desperate cries buzzes about me. They are daggers, piercing my eardrums and remaining lodged there like ugly millennial secrets. The Spanish named this cave but the voices I hear aren't speaking Spanish, one of the only two languages in my meagre repertoire. I can't make out the words, but the fear propelling each is clear. I know I am hearing the last anguished cries of those whose fate gave name to this place.

After struggling to the top of Teotihuacán's majestic Pyramid of the Sun, I crouch on the small stone terrace, exhausted. Imagining having to descend fills me with dread. As I try to quiet my heartbeat, the air fills with voices. Words I can't understand clamoring for my attention. When I am able to make peace with my lack of understanding, I find I can breach that first high step and begin my descent. But I feel I've left a lost lexicon in the tenuous air above.

In a Mexico City cloister, now a school, one voice sounds above all those from then and now. At first it bursts with poetry, then slowly grows slower and duller until its syllables fade into the very stones from which they issue. Instinctively, I know the words belong to Sor Juana: the great 17th century multilingual poet whose brilliance and feminism brought an edict of silence down upon her and who died ministering to her convent sisters during a deadly plague.

In the streets of Buenos Aires, along Zagreb's broad avenues, on Cambodia's long-silent Killing Fields, circling the kivas of Chaco's great Pueblo Bonito plaza, in the precise middle of the Friendship Bridge that once separated North and South Vietnam, in the shadow of a giant Buddha in a Burmese park, and from between the perfectly fitted stones of Peru's Sacsayhuaman, persistent voices nudge my complacency as they recite their stories of joy, grief, and pain: hellos, casual comments, whisperings of love, screams of fear, goodbyes cut down in mid-flight. Even without translation, I hear their murmurings, grasp at fragments of meaning.

It's not about translation, only witness. Not decipherment but acknowledgement. They were here. They lived. They spoke.

A child's small voice breaks through a chorus of weary talk, thin but true. All these words travel multidimensional distances—bridging time, space, death itself—to bring me the thoughts and expressions of those who uttered them, their discoveries and ideas jumping cultures to scratch my curiosity. Although translation isn't possible and I cannot know precisely what was said, I cannot ignore their insistence. They enter my dreams and offer connections, however unintelligible, telling me that humanity is one and linked in its smallest details as well as its generalities.

At Pompeii and Herculaneum, the devastating 79 AD explosion of Mount Vesuvius trapped the ultimate gestures of the approximately 2,000 people annihilated by the blast. A thick layer of ash settled on the first of those cities, lava obliterated the second. The wonders of technology eventually managed to scrape away the poisonous substances that killed those inhabitants, small holes were drilled and then injected with resin, such that we have the physical evidence of that final terrifying moment. The placement of bodies. The supplication of eyes, mouths, limbs. Even, architecture, furnishings, a lunch counter with its half-eaten meals. What we don't have is conversation. I cannot answer back.

I have never been to Pompeii or Herculaneum and it's probably too late for me now. But, judging from my experiences elsewhere, I suspect that if I were able to visit those sites, I would hear the echo of that chorus.

I want to be clear. I don't assume the voices I hear were speaking to me in their moments, an impossible conceit. They could not have imagined I would exist. But neither do I think I am eavesdropping. I prefer to believe I am paying attention to a phenomenon not yet explored by science.

The words I discern but cannot understand are not in any book. No histories record them. I have spoken with other women who also hear them, but the evidence is purely anecdotal. Ignorant of what they mean, I feel I have been given them for safekeeping.

Do I risk danger by chasing their meanings?

Figure 16

To Be or Not to Be . . . a Tourist

O verseas tourism as an activity in which great numbers of people can engage is a relatively modern concept. In the first place, because travel out of curiosity or for pleasure depends on having surplus money, something which until the mid-19th century was limited to a wealthy few. In the second, because developments in transportation made travel faster and more broadly accessible. And, also, because we tend to fear those who are different from ourselves and places that feel unfamiliar, preferring to read about them in books or watch romanticized representations on film rather than explore their reality according to what they themselves choose to tell us.

From the 17th to early 19th century, English landed aristocracy and barons of a newly established industrial class began making what they called the Grand Tour, a trip to the major cities of the European continent with an emphasis on Italy's art and culture. The name itself was telling. The Grand Tour became a rite of passage for wealthy young scions, mostly male. By mid-18th century, the Grand Tour had become a regular feature of aristocratic education in central Europe. With the 19th century rise of industrialization in the United States, the nouveau riche adapted the Tour for women as well as men (young women traveled with chaperones) and for the retired leisure class. In 1869, Mark Twain satirized the custom in his very popular book *Innocents Abroad*.

It is generally accepted that travel opens minds and erodes prejudice, but those who took the Grand Tour brought wealth and comfort with them: servants to attend to their every need, large steamer trunks filled with lavish wardrobes and accessories, trusted medications as preventives to unknown diseases, the afternoon tea or evening drink they would have enjoyed at home. When they could not make themselves understood, they simply spoke louder, a custom that sadly persists to this day.

The idea was to "do" the places they visited. Indeed, "I did Egypt" (or some other exotic locale) became the way such people spoke about those trips. The travelers rarely scratched the surface of their destinations. And the people they visited acquired an idealized sense of what life in the US was like, obtained by the travelers they met and later reaffirmed by Hollywood films.

Real adventurers were few, and almost always male. These were the seekers who had time to wander, learned other languages, experienced other ways of life, discovered ancient ruins, reached the earth's hidden places, or climbed its highest mountains. They often died in their attempts and formed an elite category no longer associated with tourism. Their fearlessness, however, did not prevent them from engaging in colonization.[16]

---

16. Although less publicized, history has also given us many women adventurers. Amelia Earhart (1897–1937) attempted to fly solo across the Pacific and died in the attempt. Freya Stark (1893–1993) visited parts of the globe few foreigners ever explore. Elizabeth Jan Cochran (also known as Nellie Bly, 1864–1922) responded to a sexist column in the Pittsburgh Dispatch by deciding to better Jules Verne's trip around the world in 80 days. She completed the journey in 72. Despite poor health, Isabella Bird (1831–1904) scaled mountains, rode thousands of miles on horseback and trekked through jungles. She became the first woman fellow (sic) in the Britain's Royal Geographical Society. And Jeanne Baret (1740–1807), disguised as a man, was the first woman to circumnavigate the globe. She joined the French Navy in 1766 as an assistant to naturalist Philibert Commerçon. It is unknown whether her true gender identity was ever discovered.

Tourism on a larger scale, including in-country destinations and accessible to an emerging upper or upper-middle class, began with the advent of mass transportation: ocean liners, national highway systems, trains, and eventually airplanes. Today the great proliferation of commercial flights is one of the biggest contributors to the pollution that is destroying our planet.

Appreciation of in-country spaces also increased. In the United States, Ulysses S. Grant signed the Yellowstone National Park Protection Act into law in 1872 and the world's first such destination was created.[17]

Tourism for working people began with the concept of the day divided into three equal parts—eight hours for work, eight for sleep, and eight for relaxation or recreation—and brought with it the idea of more modest vacations. Wage-earners might not be able to set their sights on Europe or other foreign destinations but going to recreational areas closer to home was possible and places that catered to specific groups, such as Kosher resorts in the Catskills or honeymoon packages in Hawaii proliferated.

By the end of the 20th century, tourism in its many variations, moved more people than famines or wars. This produced complex and often contradictory issues for the countries producing the travelers as well as for those receiving them. What we might call the democratization of tourism has had a tremendous global impact in terms of exchange of knowledge, ecological destruction, cultural influences, even changed families. People married those from elsewhere, and the mail-order bride came into being. Couples who couldn't adopt children in their own country sought them in

---

17. Other places of unique beauty or historical meaning soon followed: an act of Congress designated Yosemite in 1890, President McKinley declared Mount Rainier in 1899, Theodore Roosevelt Mesa Verde in 1906, and Taft Glacier in 1910, culminating to date in 63 national parks and 423 other federally protected sites. Hotels, restaurants, and concessions were established, entrance fees collected, and the national and state park systems have been popular tourist attractions ever since. This has had a mostly positive effect on the land, protecting it from industrial devastation and providing facilities that make it accessible to a broad spectrum of visitors. In isolated cases, such as Navajo National Monument in northern Arizona, control of such sites is shared with the native people who have inhabited them for millennia.

others, China and Guatemala being primary examples. While increasing person-to- person ties, this practice has also provoked problems.

Wealthier, more powerful nations have been able to impose their cultures on those that are smaller or weaker, amounting to cultural genocide in many instances. At the same time, certain destinations with extraordinary natural features (the Swiss Alps, the Riviera's beaches, Grand Canyon) or cultural draws (Shakespearean or Wagnerian festivals, Nevada's "Burning Man") have economies based on the tourists they attract. Religious sites have also proved be a major draw: Jerusalem, Mecca, and others.

At different times in history some countries have prohibited their citizens from traveling abroad. The Soviet Union rigorously controlled travel outside its borders, a limitation that wasn't reversed until 1993. When I lived in Cuba, restrictions on foreign travel were broadly enforced. Venezuela discourages its citizens from leaving the country by charging the equivalent of a year's salary for a passport. Currently, North Korea is the only country that expressly denies its citizens freedom to travel. These sorts of restrictions respond to the fear that people will discover their contemporaries live better elsewhere, and naturally promote curiosity.

In the United States we are titillated by the "other." We are curious about those who are different from ourselves, enjoying brief and highly choreographed trips to their habitats as if visiting animals in a zoo. We adapt their foods to our taste or their music to our ears and believe this reflects a sense of sophistication. We rarely learn another's language, study their histories, or attempt to understand their cultures; although there are entities such as the Summer Institute of Linguistics that have trained the best translators in the world in an effort to convert people to Christianity in the most remote places, an extremely exploitative missionary effort reminiscent of modern-day Crusades.[18]

---

18. The Summer Institute of Linguistics, a Christian evangelical institution, was founded in 1934. Its goal is to translate the Bible into every language on earth, thereby

Here at home, we may also adopt foreign artistic or religious practices, commercializing them to make them more palatable to our sensibilities. Self-styled Buddhist, Hindu, Sikh, and other gurus make millions catering to wealthy followers who prefer to stay home rather than travel to distant ashrams or teaching centers. On the purely commercial front, enterprises such as Club Med enable us to travel to other lands without ever shedding an Americanized lifestyle or coming in contact with the way those we visit really live. The world's great museums are filled with the plunder of local cultural sites.

Which is not to say that US Americans possess no genuine spirit of adventure. Exploring the "wilds" anywhere or climbing a mountain such as Everest or K2 requires courage but is almost always accomplished with the paid help of expert guides, porters who carry most of the weight, and other elements of privilege meant to ensure safety and success. In recent decades these wealthy adventure seekers have caused the deaths of innumerable guides and left tons of refuse on the slopes of Everest and other mountains.

A great many young people who have the means to do so travel to another country for a "junior college year abroad" or take what they call a gap year between high school and university. Backpacking, hitchhiking, and staying in cheap hostels help make this sort of experience possible. Those involved in such travel may dispense with many of the cautious elements so popular with adults. These youth experience undoubted benefits. They learn about other places, may make friends with locals, and believe they are participating in their ways of life. But their entitlement prevents them from making the leap. They can always return home when they tire of the unfamiliarity or discomfort. This is not to say that there aren't study abroad experiences that produce deeper connections and more lasting impressions on students of all social classes; The American

---

aiding in worldwide conversion to Christianity. In this colonialist effort, it has developed excellent translators.

Friends Service Committee and other organizations include homestays that can produce indelible ties. Still, the cultural differences and temporary nature of such experiences ultimately tend to turn them into parentheses rather than motives of lasting change.

For at least a century we have had the Peace Corps, Fulbright fellowships, a variety of religious missionary programs, Habitat for Humanity, and other such organizations that proport to aid disadvantaged peoples in other lands. Young people especially often sign onto such endeavors, sincerely believing they are doing good. Some of these organizations are better than others, or less exploitative. Too often, though, they respond to hidden political agendas aimed at gathering information or shaping policies rather than solving real problems on the ground. Rarely do they ask their supposed beneficiaries what they need or want. This is one more type of tourism that colonizes as it pretends to help. It also enables a profit-margin that has become an industry in and of itself. It is noteworthy that the US Peace Corps produced a spinoff organization calling itself Returned Volunteers, made up of those who lived the experience and denounced its true purpose.

Mass tourism—people circulating in the millions—has an incalculable impact on ecology and human health. Cruises, in which 5,000 passengers may travel on ocean liners that are like small cities, have become extremely popular. Even as they represent important profits for their ports of call, these ships use enormous amounts of energy, pollute oceans and air, and distort local cultures. With the rapid transportation made possible by airplane travel, contagious diseases are impossible to control. Witness the ways in which Covid spread from country to country despite all attempts to contain it.

Tourism can become a site of political struggle. Major events, such as the Olympics, World Cup, or any number of cultural festivals have been threatened by boycotts because the host site is in a country or state that has a draconian law against the civil rights of a particular group: women, an ethnicity, the LGBTQ+ community, or people with disabilities. In a few cases, the prospect of losing the revenue involved has even stopped such laws from being enacted.

I grew up in a family that loved to travel. My father was a public-school music teacher with three-month summer vacations. He earned a modest salary, but we also had inherited money. From my early teens, my mother, father, two younger siblings and I took summer trips to South America, Alaska, and Europe. We traveled on freighters and camped out. My parents, especially my mother, had a certain level of culture. We read about the places we went, although always in texts that told their stories from a colonial point of view. We visited museums and ancient sites. My father had a little book listing amateur string quartets in many of the places we visited, and he was sometimes able to participate in an evening of music, giving us all a closer look at the lives of those we visited.

We were more adventurous than many, although always within the conventional US American middle-class mindset. We also benefited from my mother's slightly deranged curiosity. At the time of these trips, it was customary for American citizens to register at the US embassy wherever we went. I remember officials at our embassy in Lima advising my parents not to travel to Bolivia. It was 1952, and a revolution had just taken place in that country. The very next morning Mother had us on a train headed for Lake Titicaca, followed by a crossing by boat and another train to La Paz. Mother delighted in exploring the forbidden so long as my father was willing to haul a gallon thermos of clean drinking water and she thought we would make it home again.

Like all people, though, my parents were also complex. Unaware of their patronizing attitudes, they genuinely cared about those with less. During the Second World War they "adopted" a young Dutch girl through one of those agencies that collected and distributed refugee aid. They sent her a small monthly stipend. Communication was prohibited except through the agency. But my parents were determined to find that girl and her mother and visit if they could. I remember us asking around in the small town where they lived until we showed up on their doorstep. It was a moving encounter and one that led to many years of friendship. Much later, my father invited a young Japanese musician to live with us and she became like a third daughter to him. His impulses were kind and generous, his understanding of the forces at play in such situations necessarily naïve.

I inherited my parents' curiosity about other peoples, lands, cultures, customs. Because of my desire and the course my life took, my early adulthood led me to places where I would live for years rather than visit for days, and most of my additional travel was for work. I also sought more in-depth information about the places I visited. I lived in Mexico for eight years, Cuba for eleven, and Nicaragua for almost four. I traveled to North Vietnam at the end of the American occupation and division of that country, and to Peru, Chile, and Venezuela to interview women and help publicize their stories.

Much later, with the woman who would become my lifetime companion and wife, I was privileged to travel for pleasure, visiting some of the world's great cultural sites—Angkor Wat, Petra, Rapa Nui, the Mayan world, Machu Picchu, Egypt's pyramids, the Acropolis, and others. I am fortunate to have been able to experience wild animals in their native environments in Kenya, Tanzania, Botswana, Namibia, and Zimbabwe. Such contact makes it possible for me to rail against zoos where animals live in captivity. For the millions of people who have never been on an African safari, zoos provide the singular opportunity to see such animals in the flesh. And I have been intrigued by the attitudes other travelers have demonstrated toward local people and their art; I find their tendency to always try to bargain for a lower price outrageous in the context of what the amount means to those spending and those receiving.

Here in the United States, I have hiked to ancient ruins and run the Colorado River through Grand Canyon. But point of view is always determined by privilege. I am conscious of why I have been able to have such extraordinary experiences and am immensely grateful for them.

Today there is a worldwide movement toward what we call responsible tourism. We are more than ever aware about the dangers humans pose to a fragile ecology. The expression "Take only pictures, leave only footprints" probably originated with Chief Seattle of the Suquamish and Duwamish peoples who, in the mid 1860s, made a speech in which he said: "Take only memories, leave nothing but footprints."[19] And even footprints can be destructive as they may destroy the cryptobiotic soil that takes between 20 and 250 years to reestablish itself. Whether taking photographs or memories, we know we must care for the earth, that it is not a sustainable resource if we continue to abuse it. But such consciousness of the need for care is still incipient and resultant practices vastly inadequate. As with so many other issues, it seems easier to care for our habitat than to respect the dignity and lifestyles of those we have never been taught to consider our equals.

The key to evaluating our impact on other lands and peoples is to ask those peoples themselves how tourism (read: encroachment) affects them. Still, their answers may be skewed by the commercial aspect of such tourism. As the saying goes, "our credit cards are welcome everywhere." Native populations may resent foreign influence, yet depend on the money it brings in. Practices aimed at protecting the environment may also have a contradictory impact. In 2016, when Barak Obama proposed designating a wild and beautiful area of Utah Bears Ears National Monument, there was a mixed response from local people. Some supported the protection they believed would result. Others feared increased tourism would destroy their relatively untouched part of the world.

And the concept of what constitutes "our world" keeps expanding. In 1966, the wildly popular television series Star Trek introduced each episode with the words: "To boldly go where no man has gone before." Despite

19. The origin of the adage is also attributed to Robert Baden-Powell who was the founder of the Scout movement and to John Muir who founded the Sierra Club.

troubling the grammarians, and feminists who resented limiting the phrase to the males of our species, it characterizes humanity's intrepid desire for conquest. In 1969 an astronaut set foot on the moon for the first time.[20] The US space program now has its sights on Mars. And a wealthy few are currently spending thousands for a few minutes of experiencing sub-orbital weightlessness.

Do we travel to learn or conquer, to visit, give, appropriate, or simply satisfy our curiosity? Can we see the other when educated and conditioned to think of ourselves as superior? Whatever our answers to these questions, a consciousness of colonization begs our attention. And even in this era in which many museums are returning stolen treasures to their places of origin, it behooves us to look at how our biases may be colonizing such acts of decolonization.

---

20. The Soviets landed an unmanned spacecraft to the moon in 1959 but it wasn't until a decade later, on July 20, 1969, that a manned craft reached the destination. Neil Armstrong and Buzz Aldrin explored the moon's surface for about two and a half hours, collecting rock specimens and making observations. Armstrong's initial announcement, "That's one step for a man, one giant step for mankind," continues to sound a clarion call for the idea of ultimate conquest.

Gaps
—for Robert Cohen

*D*o you remember the name *of the town she took us to for a picnic—* *and then showed us the hidden Nahua calendar stone she was deciphering for the local community?* My partner for eight years and father of my youngest child was asking me about our friend Laurette Sejourné. During my years in Mexico, we saw one another often and she generously shared her archeological adventures. I have often thought about that time, dreamed about it, written its dramas in poetry and prose.

What an exceptional moment that picnic must have been. But no, I don't remember. It and so many other moments have long since fallen between the tired folds of my brain. I wonder where they live now. I cannot imagine it simply evaporated, but rather that it exists just as the bodies of the disappeared in Latin America's dirty wars of the 1970s and '80s exist in unmarked graves, just out of reach of their comrades and loved ones.

My youngest child just celebrated her 53rd birthday, and the time to which my ex-partner was referring is at least that long ago. I remember many prior picnics with Laurette, savored at the Teotihuacan site she later called the Palace of the Butterflies, an area where the inhabitants of that ancient city once lived in rows of small houses. I even remember the lunches she would prepare and bring in an old-fashioned wicker basket: roast chicken, pâtés of various sorts, fruits, cheeses, at least two kinds of bread. Their scents still inhabit the echo chamber of my memory. I remember my friend's face, especially her dark intense eyes, so wise and curious.

I can imagine how special it must have been for the community whose name I have forgotten to learn how their ancestors counted the days. And for me to have watched as the brilliant archeologist searched for ways to transmit their history to those to whom it belonged. But the privilege of my own connection to that experience is gone from my consciousness.

As far as I know, I don't suffer from Alzheimer's or any other type of dementia. At least not yet. My memory functions as one might expect in an 87-year-old. I read and write and drive and travel and cook and clean and dress myself without help. And when I do forget a name or word, if I leave a blank and move on, I can usually retrieve it without too much delay.

I'm talking about something less critical but insistent enough to warrant examination. Friends may bring up a moment or person, perhaps an incident we shared, and one that obviously holds meaning for them. I search my memory for my image of the moment. Nothing is there. I may remember other moments with the same person or place, just not the one mentioned. Or I may not even recall the name of the person or the location of which my friend is speaking.

Why do some droplets of memory evaporate like rain when the sun has dried the earth after a storm? Why are certain pieces of the jigsaw puzzle lost forever, leaving gaping holes where they once completed a scene? What causes us to have perfect recall for seemingly unimportant incidents while others, which might have been pivotal in our lives, disappear from view? And storyteller that I am, why doesn't my imagination weave a fabric capable of linking one memory to another, smoothing over the absences on its journey to fruition?

Today I ask myself how I may be able to fill those gaps, what I might dream, imagine, or invent that would render the fabric whole? Perhaps the challenge now is to engage another sort of memory, one that emerges from the depths of our hidden places or springs from a confabulation of secrets to provide the safety net we need in these times of dangerous distraction.

The Restaurant[21]

The Roman neighborhood was beautiful but overrun by tourists. Most restaurants looked expensive. The man and woman decided to try Malatesta, a small family eatery recommended by the woman who ran their lodging. They thought it just might be named for Errico Malatesta, the Italian anarchist who loved unions, spent years in prison, and was exiled from several European countries including his own. When they arrived for an early dinner, it was crowded with locals, always a good sign.

Looking at the menu, they saw that water was free. Purchasing water was the norm everywhere they'd been so far, but here they read: *We do not charge for water, which is the right of all peoples. Yes, definitely the same Malatesta*, the woman said. They ordered a seafood starter and robust main dishes that arrived teasing the edges of oversized plates. The food was plentiful and delicious. The woman had gnocchi, prepared to perfection with loving hands. The man had ravioli stuffed with spinach and several local cheeses. Everything was fresh and home cooked. She drank a couple of glasses of good wine. Neither could resist dessert.

---

21. This text is based on a true story told to me by my son Gregory and his wife Laura.

When it was time to pay their bill, their waiter—a friendly sort who'd asked them where they were from and recommended several out of the way places which he thought they would like—didn't hand them an itemized slip of paper with tax added and suggested tip. He simply said: *That'll be 25 euros,* which they paid, astonished at how ridiculously inexpensive the meal had been.

The next night the man and woman decided to return to Malatesta. This time they ordered more than the night before. Everything was so delicious, and they could always take the leftovers back to the b&b and feast on them for lunch the next day, when the excessive heat made it uncomfortable to go out. Once again, they dined to satiation and asked for the check. This time their waiter told them they owed *20 euro.* Five less than the previous night.

I think there must be a mistake, the man said, *last night we ate less, and the check was more.* The waiter, by now practically a family member, fumbled for a moment in the manner of someone who knows he's messed up and wants to remedy the situation. Then he said: *Okay, give me 25.* Once again without a written check, the man handed over the requested amount and he and the woman walked back to where they were staying. They carried containers of what they hadn't been able to consume, the exuberant scents floating in the oppressively humid air of this dangerously hot summer.

That night the man was curious. He went online to see if he could find references to this restaurant named after an Italian anarchist, where the food was extraordinary, and the prices seemed to depend upon the server's whim.

It turned out that Malatesta was listed, with a few photographs he immediately recognized. There were many testimonials from diners who had eaten there. All agreed that the food was superb. Several remarked on how inexpensive it was. But one client's comment stood out from the rest. He said the food was delicious, although the prices seemed a bit high: he'd paid 37 euros for a single dish!

The waiter must not have liked this guy, the man told the woman, *he says the food was great but expensive.* She smiled.

What kind of a world might we live in if services rendered were charged according to how much or how little the provider liked the client? A commodity culture would become one of friendly exchange overnight. I'm willing to bet that kindness would soon replace the dry businesslike give and take symptomatic of the life we've created for ourselves, and that we'd notice an immediate improvement in collective mood.

Anomaly or Foreshadowing

On August 15, 2022, a news story in the New York Times reported that they began distributing menstrual products free in Scotland, the first country in the world to tackle *period poverty*, as the inability to buy those items has been called.[22] Similar laws are under review in several other countries and in a number of US states. Acknowledgment of such a need surfaced during Covid, when many young women especially found themselves in quarantine and thus unable to leave the house to buy the products they needed, or out of work and too poor to afford them.

Perhaps this will also help to lessen *period shame*, the discomfort absurdly associated with that natural phenomenon experienced monthly by almost all women between the ages of twelve and fifty. Men, especially, are reluctant to shop for such products. As I understand it, Scots can go to an online app to find places where the items are dispensed, including public libraries, schools and universities, pharmacies, and supermarkets. In the latter locations they may select what they need from the shelves but won't have to pay for them when they reach checkout.

---

22. "Scotland Makes Period Products Free" by Remy Tumin, New York Times, August 15, 2022

The news is startling in several ways. In the first place, any item of recurrent use that is made freely available in our consumer societies is a surprise. In the second, we women are not accustomed to commerce recognizing, much less accommodating, our needs. All sorts of items for women are more expensive than their counterparts for men. When it comes to gender-specific medical conditions, insurance companies as well as the entire for-profit health system punishes us in comparison with our fathers, husbands, brothers, sons. As just one example, medication for erectile disfunction is covered by most health insurance policies while birth control pills, if they are available at all, are not.

We may also be surprised by this news because in Scotland, as in so many countries, free menstrual products may not be the most pressing measure on the long road to gender equality. In 2021 the median hourly wage for women was 11.6 percent less than for men. And that's just one example out of the hundreds of ways in which it's easier in that country to be male than female. Why free tampons, we might ask?

It's possible to chalk misogyny in product availability and cost up to the general misogyny we women face in society. Men have long been favored when it comes to the easy availability of what they need or want. But there must be something else at play here because women, after all, are the big shoppers, those who buy for every population group. Most often than not, we are the ones who shop for our family's food, our children's clothing, and our household's cleaning products. Men may purchase more of the big-ticket items such as homes and cars, but it's we women who rack up those repeat purchases, day after day.

I might conclude that Scotland, perhaps because those leading that country today are more justice-oriented, really do have women's needs at heart. Or perhaps one of that country's legislators got the idea for the bill, introduced the idea, and then managed to drum up enough support to get it passed. Essential or fortuitous, it's a welcome move.

Menstruation has traditionally been feared in many cultures. A natural process that wasn't broadly understood caused misunderstanding and suspicion, especially in men who typically established the social norms. Since widespread knowledge of human reproduction is rather recent in our history, perhaps there was a strange logic to that fear. In some parts of the world, when they had their periods, women were isolated from mainstream society, even forced to distance themselves in special huts built for the purpose. In others, menstruating women were not allowed to handle food.

Even today menstruation continues to generate a certain aura of mystery. Women of menstrual age who live together have noticed that their periods occur at the same time, a phenomenon called *period synchronicity*. They claim there is something about their pheromones, the moon's gravitational pull, and oceanic tides that align their calendars; the younger stronger women pulling the others into their cycles. The medical field tends to discredit this, and studies have been inconclusive.

The *virgin or whore* dichotomy has long been the paradigm making it easy for male-dominated forces to either put women on pedestals that do us no good at all or punish us for our gender.

In the United States, a recent catastrophic example of women being forced to bend to right-wing rule was the Supreme Court decision reversing Roe v. Wade. A law for which we fought hard for generations and from which we benefited for almost half a century, was overturned by a dictatorial president installing three lifetime justices who during their confirmation hearings lied under oath about their attitudes toward abortion. The arrogant verdict prevents women from exercising control over their own bodies, including the important decision of whether or when to give birth. Thousands of women have already been victimized by this reversal as state after state implements egregious restrictions on a woman's right to choose.

The new battlefield has also returned some surprises, though. In Kansas, a conservative state where Donald Trump won by almost fifteen percentage points in 2020, 59 percent of the electorate voted against the new restrictions. This means that, at least for now, abortion will remain legal in the state, encouraging voters nationwide to follow its example of political education and organization. During the 2022 midterms, several other states enacted protective measures.

History teaches us that when classist, racist, and misogynist governments move against us, we must find different and more creative ways of struggling for justice. I hope that one day it will cease to be necessary for us to judge progress for more than half the number of humans by these small steps or isolated measures. I suspect that will only be possible, though, when power is equitably distributed among all genders. Will that ever happen?

In the context of the routine and ongoing inequality that governs women's lives, Scotland's commitment to our needs is interesting. Should we consider it an anomaly among nations, an advanced measure, or a foreshadowing of victories to come?

Vanishment

o vanish is a verb that carries the mystery and energy of a noun. Vanishment. It presupposes the one-time existence of something no longer there. We have an afterimage or echo. The memory of what was informs what is.

A hologram is not an alternative to something that has vanished, because an event or scene is being created from computerized knowledge of its characteristics, only partially possible today but surely an everyday occurrence in a rapidly approaching future. Neither is the construction of something imagined or the shadow made by a form we may not see but that exists, lengthening and foreshortening as the sun moves across the sky.

Vanishing bequeaths a memory, and yet memory, too, depends upon the mind of the person experiencing its gift. We remember some things as if they happened yesterday, some only in the broken shards produced by trauma, some with the haze of age or thorniness of regret. We are often required to meet memory halfway. Those who have been abused will remember differently from those who abused them. A way of life has vanished for the first while the second appropriated that way of life and their memories drip with self-serving excuses.

There was a time when the United States was known throughout the world as a democracy, a nation that was founded and had grown with a sense of fairness around individual freedoms, and with a legal system that insured those freedoms for anyone. Well, not really for anyone. If you are descended from this land's original inhabitants or from Africans kidnapped and brought here as slaves . . . if you love someone of your own gender or your gender was misdiagnosed at birth . . . if you have the misfortune to lack a home . . . if you are a woman . . . if you defend ideas unapproved by the mainstream, those much-advertised democratic freedoms are not so readily available. But, well, for anyone else . . . Who is those who make up that category *anyone else*? Are they perpetrators by default?

Those who vanished did so not of their choosing. Many, defying their murderers, insisted on survival. Majorities were kidnapped, separated from their loved ones, infected with unfamiliar diseases, raped, starved, worked to death, and then lied about.

The idea of a nation founded out of nothing was the first lie.

The vanishing has been slow and subtle. Here and abroad, all those peoples our democracy has invaded and occupied, exploited, and crippled, and used to benefit its rapacious gluttony—understood it long before we who reap the specious benefits did. In Latin America, especially during the Dirty Wars of the 1970s and '80s but continuing in lesser numbers today, vanishment acquired a new name: disappearance. Tens of thousands who fought dictatorial regimes were taken from their homes and quite literally disappeared. The lack of a body that might have provided closure to loved ones, was its own sort of torture. It has taken us a while to catch up. Some have never done so.

Some vanishments leave no trace. We must approach them blindfolded and guess what they have in mind. And beware of verbs that were once nouns. They can grab you and never let go.

Death

uman history has recorded death in different ways. The Egyptians believed their dead traveled to another realm and provided them with everything they would need for the journey: food, utensils, cash. Throughout the world, many cultures followed this custom of burying goods with their dead. Consequently, grave robbing has become an industry. When they remove the buried items, are the robbers really depriving the dead of what they will need to live well on the other side? Or are they only making a profit from stealing priceless relics that have no real connection with a dubious afterlife?

Greek mythology gave us the river Styx, a word that means *shuddering* and expresses a loathing of death. Charon was the ferryman who rowed the souls of the deceased across. In payment he received the coins that were placed in each corpse's mouth. Certain Indian sects buried brides along with their dead husbands. Mormons say that if a man is married by the church's laws he will be reunited after death with his wife and will rule his very own planet. Male dreams are so often about domination. Religions and cultures create belief systems that incorporate such ideas about the spiritual and even physical nature of life after death.

To a non-believer such as myself, these assumptions are fantasy. Yet billions of educated adults adhere to one or another version of what they can expect once our life on earth is done. It isn't hard to understand the human quest for some sort of continuance. We give so much—hope, thought, energy—to the years we have; many cannot accept that they will end, and nothing at all will endure.

Because these diverse perspectives are so important to those who hold them, the transition between life and death observes detailed rituals in a diversity of cultures. Jews must bury their dead within 24 hours, and the body, which is not embalmed, is washed according to scripture before being wrapped in a cotton shroud and placed in a plain pine coffin. Mourners then sit shiva for seven days. Shava sadhana is a tantric practice in which adepts meditate sitting on a corpse. Strict rules apply, beginning with the selection of the corpse. Catholic mythology imagines sweet little angels, and artists throughout time have portrayed them in paintings and on church walls. Catholics, Muslims, Buddhists, and others each follow their own observances as life gives way to death.

These male-oriented customs spawn requirements, practices, and industries. In the United States, the mortuary and funeral businesses are enormous money-makers, and billions are spent each year on preparing the body for viewing, acquiring the receptacle—coffin or urn—purchasing the cemetery plot and gravestone, and tending the burial site. It can cost more to be dead than to be alive. Many US Americans extend such practices to their pets, who are given funerals and buried in special plots in the company of others of their species. In recent years, ecological and space concerns have introduced what many consider more ecologically sound practices, such as *green burial*. Given the consumerist nature of our society, these too have gotten more and more expensive.

I am less interested in these elaborate rituals than I am in what happens when we die. Is it possible that the powerful life force simply ceases to exist? Science tells us that energy doesn't end but only changes form. Numerous people describe experiences in which they died and returned to life. Many tell stories of a bright light at the end of a tunnel and the appearance of dear ones who preceded them in death and who are now waiting to welcome them to the other side. Repetition of this storyline is taken as proof that it is a legitimate narrative.

Death is one of those events which, although inevitable, seems distant and vague when we are young, looming more immanent as we grow older. Youth by its very nature is accompanied by a sense of immortality. As visible attributes—skin, muscle, eyesight, hearing, energy, stamina, and the capacity to recover from illness or injury—begin to change, the idea of the end feels more real, possibly too close for comfort. I cannot remember wondering about dying before I was in my sixties or seventies. Now I do so frequently, but it involves more curiosity than dread.

A dear friend, a poet whose voice I believe and sensibility I respect, experienced death and returned. His heart stopped beating for 20 minutes. Fortunately, he was in his doctor's office at the time, and medical revival was accessible. They massaged his chest and got his heart started again. When he came to, he was very tired. He reported no tunnel or light, nor had he been greeted by anyone he knew. Still, the experience affected him deeply. It changed his approach to life, his priorities, his poems. But it didn't tell me anything about dying that induces me to adopt any of the beliefs put forth by religion or social custom.

In fact, when it comes to the variety of beliefs about what happens when we die, the idea of a system itself is what bothers me. I understand that such systems and the beliefs they embrace have been developed as control mechanisms and/or moneymakers. It's the very invention of a system that seems absurd to me, even arrogant. Life and death are profound journeys. I think we must respect them in all their wonder, without attempting to dress them in the ridiculous or impossible.

Regarding death, the thing we can be sure about is that it is final. We live, and then we die. Which tells me that we must make the most of every living moment, doing our best to be the person we want to be. Afterwards, who knows? If it turns out there is something more, it would be a plus.

The Future

The future is like rain. It can be gentle and refreshing or a destructive flood. It might descend in torrents, but by the time we look out the window the sky is clear. The storm has passed. Only sleek streets, wet soil and dripping leaves remain. The world looks clean, but that may be an illusion. We cannot see where the earth has loosened, threatening all we have built upon it. The future becomes the past before we've had time to catch up.

Like all children, I believed my parents and the way they lived mirrored the world. The future would bring more of the same. If I learned to get along, I would do all right. I joined church and Masonic youth groups that embarrassed my mother and father, had them crossing streets without looking in both directions. Later I would have to depart those groups in shame.

I laced my saddle shoes from top to bottom, fingers crossed behind my back. I mimicked the popular kids, danced to the unrelenting rhythms of Country & Western, and cried myself to sleep as I clutched a worn photo of my high school's basketball team, the face I kissed all but worn through by my longing. A friend of my parents gave me a small leather pouch containing a twenty-dollar bill. *In case of emergency*, she said. Adults assured me it would get better. One day the future would come.

I married the first man who offered to take me from that world which, by then, I realized was neither mine nor the only one there was. The marriage didn't last, but it started me on a journey of my making. I found my mentors: more important than most relationships defined by blood. They showed me I could participate in a different future, one that made sense for everyone. Art and revolution quickened my breath.

Future tense is always precarious. We have expectations, hopes, believe we are on the winning side. It was obvious that health and education and work were things humanity needed and wanted, so we struggled relentlessly for them. We fervently wanted justice to prevail. Oh, we knew some of us wouldn't live to see it. But that was the price we'd have to pay, and we forged ahead: young, innocent, and willing. Those dreams flooded our eyes, blinding us to our own mistakes as well as to enemy deception.

Where we arrived is completely different.

The past leaves an indelible mark. Even when written in invisible ink. I remember wanting to ask a question but falling silent before such aggressive power plays. I was tired and it was easier to go along. And then too I believed, believed, believed. It's too late now to go back and do it over. Past and present taunt one another like water and oil—no wonder both are diminishing resources in a world that resolves every issue violently. The questions have been forgotten. No one else echoed my hesitation back then, and I didn't raise my hand. My lack of confidence carved a place where one thing led to another. Eventually, things turned ugly.

Today is a place I don't recognize.

My future accompanies me now but suffers from a strange malady. It is populated by my children and their descendants: all healthy, all playing instruments emitting wondrous music. Astonishment is a never-ending season. The woman I love loves me. But outside my window deep crevices open across the land, swallowing all the yesterdays. City streets fill with the refuse of war and debris of effort. The ghosts of those who sacrificed themselves speak a language I cannot forget.

We are in the habit of believing the future is far off, so distant it may never arrive. We hold up pictures that depict it dressed in Easter morning colors, evidence of failures intoning a chorus of *what ifs*. A rebel echo haunts my days and invades my dreams with tender memories.

I will always be proud that we tried.

Survival in Defeat

The victim who is able to articulate
the situation of the victim
has ceased to be a victim.
He or she has become a threat.
  —James Baldwin

We need a way to celebrate defeat, the tragedy of my generation and several succeeding ones. Or if not celebrate it, at least not let it destroy us. Celebrating victory comes replete with exuberant acts—the adoration of a grateful public, high praise, resounding anthems, ostentatious parades, glittering medals—many of these responses verging on hypocrisy or descending into the breast-beating demagoguery of false patriotism, guaranteed to drag young and old alike into attitudes that distort the deepest meanings of being human.

Not long after 1989, when the Soviet Union imploded, the Berlin Wall came down, and the socialist world in general crumbled beneath the avalanche of capitalism's win, my son said: *Because we lost, no one knows our dead. Had we won, streets would bear their names and monuments to their courage would be everywhere.* It wasn't an idle comment about men and women who were strangers to us. We'd both given years of our lives to the struggle and lost close friends. Some in the torture chambers of various dictatorships, some gunned down in uneven battles or in the streets, some simply disappeared, their final resting places forever undisclosed.

In 2003 my friend, the brilliant human rights lawyer Jules Lobel, published a book called *Success without Victory*.[23] In it he discusses the unsuccessful legal efforts by abolitionist lawyers to free fugitive slaves through the courts, Susan B. Anthony's trial for voting illegally as a woman, the post-Civil War challenges to segregation that resulted in the courts' later affirmation of the separate but equal doctrine in Plessy v. Ferguson and eventually to Brown v. Board of Education, as well as Lobel's own challenges to US foreign policy during the 1980s and '90s. All those legal battles were lost but paved the way for important future victories. In that sense they might be judged successful although they didn't result in immediate victory. They showed us that the processes leading to eventual wins often take unexpected turns.

When things first fell apart, those who devoted lifetimes of struggle to achieving more just societies often tried to console ourselves by emphasizing that we might have lost a battle but not the war. Now we must admit, to ourselves most painfully, that we've indeed lost the war. At least for the foreseeable future. International capital showed its superior power and reach. We probably won't live to see history's pendulum swing back in the other direction. Our children and grandchildren might not live to see it either.

And of course, we wonder if the pendulum will swing back. Can our defeat have been so definitive that our beautiful dreams of inclusion and equality have become a notion that humanity might entertain only as some impossible fairy tale? If the answer is yes, unspeakable sacrifice will have been in vain.

---

23. New York City, NY: New York University Press.

These are questions only time will answer. Perhaps my generation's losses will, in fact, pave the way for future successes. Those brutal defeats have led to processes that have resulted in progressive governments in some countries. Bolivia and Chile come to mind.

But that's not my concern here. I'm dealing with something far more immediate. I want to know how we, who were defeated in our quest for socialism, can remain viscerally proud of efforts that ended in failure. How we may continue to feel good about struggles that cost so much without achieving their goals. And, perhaps most urgently, how we ourselves avoid giving in to the victor's specious claim that a society based on competition and strongarm tactics equals progress.

In 1989, many of us involved in the revolutionary struggles of the 1960s to '80s experienced a kind of shared depression. By then we knew the socialist model wasn't all we'd hoped it would be. We recognized the problems, could see the cracks. But we supported socialism not only because we believed in its promises but as a balance to capitalist hegemony. If that balance was lost, we knew we were lost.

And then it was, and we were.

How could we extricate ourselves from the lethargy of despair and regain collective and individual agency: as feeling and functioning human beings, as thinkers, as creative people capable of looking reality in the face and imagining another future. I wanted once again to get up each morning and go to my writing desk filled with curiosity and the energy to work. It was the human edge of the problem that gnawed at us and that concerns me here.

Healing means learning to relax into more authentic versions of ourselves. It means dispensing with a malignant sectarianism. It means privileging process and imagination. It means asking questions we'd failed to ask and opening ourselves to ideas that required broadening our understanding of who the experts are. It means humility, an unfamiliar trait for people who once arrogantly believed we possessed all the answers.

I can only speak for myself. My journey has been torturous at times. My sense of personal failure often translated itself into apathy or unbearable sadness. The ghosts of my many dead visited when I least expected them, wondering what their sacrifices meant. Their imploring faces sometimes made me want to run and hide: Haydée Santamaría, José Benito Escobar, Carlos Fonseca, Miguel Enríquez, Kathy Boudin. Although Ernesto "Che" Guevara wasn't someone I knew personally, his 1967 defeat and execution was the prelude to the overall defeat of a multifaceted movement.

I had to find a way to come up for air. And I wanted it to be genuine, one that doesn't involve justification or making vain excuses.

Gradually, over a period of several years, my ghosts settled in their graves. As the doctor and Chilean revolutionary leader Bautista Van Schouwen told his captors in 1973: *You don't know why you torture me, but I know why I die.* The values of justice and equality that had motivated me took precedence over the fact that I hadn't succeeded in helping to install egalitarian societies in my lifetime. My comrades and I achieved pockets of progress and created moments of justice that improved some lives in the here and now and may serve as examples to those who will struggle more successfully in the future.

I think about the cruel war launched by the United States against Vietnam when I was a young adult. That conflagration had a defining impact on my developing political consciousness. Long after the Vietnamese reclaimed their nation, veterans on both sides began meeting to get to know one another and try to heal their psychic wounds. It's never only about a conflict in terms of winning and losing, but about your throat constricting, your breath quickening, a general feeling of numbness getting in the way of your ability to move ahead, and your memory becoming permanently damaged: the physical feelings that defeat generates and our capacity as humans to overcome their limitations and survive.

I am surviving in defeat, and it no longer feels only like loss.

Ghost

G host attempts to still the confusion surrounding her every gesture. Even at the age she was when she died, she isn't prepared for the responsibilities she instinctively knows lie ahead. And what does age mean now? It hardly translates. All she knows, with a certainty locked beneath her breastbone and safe in her conviction, is the perfect storm of words birthed by her energy of experience, getting it down on paper and sending it out into the world.

She notices herself casting about for the catch and release of story. She misses the click of connection as each piece finds its niche in the labyrinth of her imagination, then remembers the power of the search itself: discovery of language as more than a tool of communication and growing wonder as she learned to move her words into unique patterns, explosions doing what she intended. How a comma lit the night sky one October 2nd, or an explanation point became superfluous when we wept in unison and craft ceded to feeling. *There's nothing new under the sun* was a meaningless adage in her repertoire of learning.

Pay attention, but not too much attention. Frightening people belongs in those tales about the supernatural that are written by the living. Try to get used to going out and about by night as well as day. Repeated invitations of unexplored horizons. A brightly lit stage compensates for the embarrassment that inevitably attends shadowy sightings.

It isn't easy when she's pierced by the high back of a sudden chair or floats effortlessly through a closed door without the thump or bruising that such encounters produced when she lived. And all too easy to dissolve in shame or become lost in such random accidents. Everything was ponderous back then, weighted by the immensity of corporality, bound by laws that would fragment as understanding replaced superstition. But weightlessness can be problematic as well. It's hard to hold on with grace.

Her disabilities chuckle and assert themselves, no longer limiting mobility. Proceeding deliberately was always more effective than speed. Form and color devour center stage. Race is neither skin deep nor, it turns out, resides in any melting pot. It simply shouts its name with pride or inhabits silence with an attitude born of resistance. All genders weigh the same on these trays hanging from chains sustained by work-weary hands. And mundane answers to the question of what, if anything, happens after death seem irrelevant.

At first, when close enough to old friends that she can reach out and touch them, she can't help but feel hurt by their lack of response. Her new acquaintances tell her not to take the perceived slights personally. This is a different space, buoyed by larger questions, a season for every need. It will take some getting used to. She learns that some choose to return from time to time, showing up when least expected to help a stranger in need. Some call such apparitions ghosts; others call them angels.

And the words still fill her mouth, keeping her company when she feels most alone. They tell her magic exists and shout *game on* when conditions require that she make a point. This magic she was born to and for which she died refuses to relinquish its power.

Invisible mirrors tell her she loves how she looks. All she need do is imagine herself trailing the billowing gossamer of teal chiffon with wild flowing hair to match or dressed in an elegantly cut gray-black suit and carrying a briefcase costing more than any accessory she'd possessed in life, and there she is: sheathed in her dream of the moment and ready to take on the world. Regal nakedness also brings occasional delight, the perfect posture of pride. It may take time without measure for her to understand the world she left behind was mostly blind to this reality.

There is the significant matter of a name. She tries on one after another, conscious she can pick and choose now, trading them out on whim. In life, a name had serious, often static, implications. You adapted to the one you were given or chose one with which you felt comfortable. Representation as identity. Social strictures determined how you might be addressed: from *little girl* to *cutie pie* or *hey there* and finally *miss*, *missus*, or *ms*, depending on age and milieu. Here the language of acknowledgment seems as irrelevant as failing to make direct eye contact or offer a firm handshake.

At first her current home seems too big, walls too porous, floor too unstable, roof rotted through in places and weather unsure. She longs for the cocoon of her last nest, the one she shared with the woman she loved for thirty-seven precious years. She can attest to the fact that one never really appreciates what one has until it's gone. This newfound freedom to come and go is disarming, sometimes disconcerting. The vanity of temperature as well. Now she is never too hot or too cold. Rather than a pleasurable turn of events, this feels like a liability at times, a painful reminder she's no longer among the living.

The loving made everything possible. That amazement of their connection. And her lost words echo as they flee, deserting hope, sculpting sorrow. This is the only real issue, what matters most. Changing out one word for another. All that work to be able to write to the rhythm of her desire. All that pruning and honing, taking terrifying risks, peeling away what didn't fit, exposing what hurt or shamed, reorganizing for ultimate focus and impact.

Yesterday wind roared and the threat of wildfire was everywhere. Today, more than a foot of snow glistens outside her roaming place. In the world where she left her breath, it was only discernible to herself, might have steamed the inside surface of a windowpane. And her finger, if not frozen in horror, might have inscribed a message on the momentary palette. That none of this could happen now only reinforces her sense of isolation.

Memory is key, and she struggles to retain what seems to fragment and dissolve even as she strains to lock it in. To store it in ready tears and stoic cells. If she can remember the gentle comfort of her beloved's hand, the balm of her lips, her ability to find the missing word or provide an end to a sentence trailing into fog, the words may return. If she can dream of nestling once more in her generosity of spirit. Then it may be possible for her to curl her body beneath the blanket that adorned the bed they shared.

The faces of her children, grandchildren, and great grandchildren flash before her unfocussed eyes. If only she could recall their names. She still holds the reins that guided them into worlds of their own even as she knew she had to let them go, trust their diverse creativities. An intensity of desert heat calms her erratic heartbeat. A dramatic red rock wall against the vastness of blue. A perfect claret cup bloom opening in early morning light.

She almost appreciates this absence of tension, no vehement opinions careening across a sea of resignation. No urgent struggle demanding her involvement. No ballistics of regret. No war to be won or lost because she shows up or doesn't. Almost, but not entirely. The words of her poem disappear as soon as she tries to write them down. Permanence is liquid now. What is most unsettling is that none of this matters. Or does it? Moving in any direction, she only succeeds in getting out of her own way.

Slowly, she begins to make new friends. Ghosts like herself. They appear from different times and places. One plump and affable grandmotherly type comes around in the late afternoons, brandishing a brightly colored fan as if it were a weapon, regardless of weather. A lean young trans man sometimes nestles against her lonely ribs, his resolute energy imbuing her with courage. A small girl reminds her of her child self, eyes glistening with future. A wise old elephant, its wrinkled trunk reaching in friendly anticipation. A baobab tree drawing her into the safety of its vast trunk or willow sheltering her beneath its branches.

Is that Hypatia of Alexandria caressing a cup of mint tea in the remoteness of antiquity? Harriet Tubman struggling to wake from a sudden bout of narcolepsy? Ingrid Bergman weighing mystery in one hand, Hollywood in the other? Chief Seattle talking back to Barack Obama with all of history on his side? Emma Goldman dancing beyond the edges of revolution. An unnamed child perched on a curb, deep in her discovery of feeling. None of them are in a hurry. Forever is etched on all their foreheads. As each appears or retreats, she knows she will see them again whenever she feels the need of their company. Continuous community.

Then, without warning, something resembling lightning strikes. Its force is greater than anything she's experienced, in the now or before. As if time is suddenly rent by a perfect storm of circumstance or intensity of desire, everything shifts. Not in violence but with a subtlety that defies the rules of physics. Perhaps that sliver of a moment known as *the leap second* has somehow escaped its fabric of continuity. Perhaps it is she herself who has breached some barrier, undergone irreconcilable change.

Colors are reversed. Yellow becomes green, blue red. Triangles transform themselves into circles, squares into French horns. A musical scale never heard before overcomes her ears. She tries to cover them with open palms, but her flesh fails to prevent the clash. Ancient rhythms course through her nerves and musculature. Space opens its mouth but cannot swallow. The labor pains of monumental birth shake her translucent body, protected by integrity alone.

Without any real conviction about her current state, crossing this bridge that stretches out before her isn't possible. She can neither decipher nor analyze the moment and knows she needn't try. Looking around, no one else seems troubled by the fork in the road. Choosing left or right will make no difference. Up and down are equally benign.

For an instant, she wishes she were back on familiar ground, sure of her small place and direction. In life the need to choose was often daunting, producing angst in the throat and a shortness of breath. A decision, once made, only pointed forward. Now her growing awareness that an option may not be what it seems fills her with momentary dread. But as she moves in one direction and then another, she understands it isn't where she places herself so much as what she sees with her eyes closed and how she navigates the terrain. There will always be choices to be made. Risk remains a constant. Something resembling relief floods this amorphous displacement of air.

Itinerate, with neither gender nor nation, she settles into herself. Shooting stars whistle past her ears. Resistance lies exhausted at the water's edge. A voice beyond any octave she's inhabited sings her to sleep in millennial quiet. Her skin becomes flawless again, her hair voluminous: sparse white returning to vibrant chestnut. Her eyes regain their youthful blue and widen in anticipation.

The verb *to be* may rise to meet us as default, but one truth appears with absolute certainty: without the making and doing, simply being is never enough. Not in our fragile past or impossible future. Not while we live or even in that legacy which we deposit in the memories of those we leave behind.

And so, she understands. She stands upright and takes confident strides, perfectly balanced on the cusp of her own goodbye: Love, powerful as it is, only survives the line between life and death if both people let go, forgive, remember. Its endurance depends on both parts. What doesn't die is what you make with passion and tenacity. No metaphor describes this reality, only untiring passion carrying our creativity on its wings.

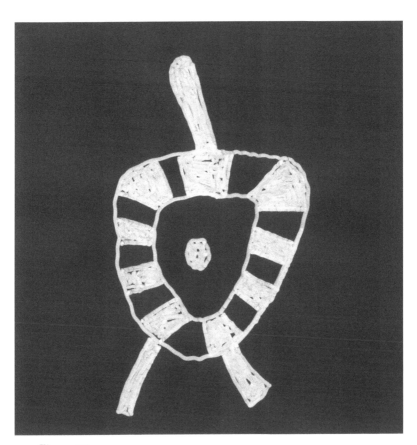

Figure 17

Barbara Byers' Note About Her Drawings
Petroglyphs

I have been in love with petroglyphs all through the Southwest. I have for many years drawn them as a way of trying to understand the expressions they give. This work is to honor their presence in the world.

Petroglyphs are figures chipped into rocks by the various Native peoples who have been in this area for a really long time. My figures are not meant to be translations, especially by non-native artists. I just have a deep love for them.

The images in this book are white acrylic pen on black paper. The drawings are approximately 4″ × 4″. They do not illustrate the text. Margaret and I enjoy working together in this way.

About Margaret Randall

Margaret Randall (New York, 1936) is a poet, essayist, oral historian, translator, photographer, and social activist. She lived in Latin America for twenty-three years (in Mexico, Cuba, and Nicaragua). From 1962 to 1969 she and Mexican poet Sergio Mondragón co-edited *El Corno Emplumado /
The Plumed Horn*, a bilingual literary quarterly that published some of the best new work of the sixties. When she came home in 1984, the government ordered her deported because it found some of her writing to be "against the good order and happiness of the United States". With the expertise of The Center for Constitutional Right and support of many writers and others, she won her case, and her citizenship was restored in 1989.

Randall's most recent poetry titles include *Against Atrocity, Out of Violence Into Poetry* (both from Wings Press), *Stormclouds Like Unkept Promises, Vertigo of Risk*, and *Home* (all from Casa Urraca Press). *Che On My Mind* (a feminist poet's reminiscence of Che Guevara) and *Haydée Santamaría, Cuban Revolutionary: She Led by Transtression* (both published by Duke University Press), *Thinking About Thinking* (essays, from Casa Urraca), and *My Life in 100 Objects* and *Artists in My Life* (New Village Press) are other recent titles. In 2020 Duke brought out her memoir, *I

Never Left Home: Poet, Feminist, Revolutionary. A second selected poems, *Time's Language II,* will be issued by Wings in fall 2023.

Two of Randall's photographs are in the Capitol Art Collection in Santa Fe. She has also devoted herself to translation, producing *When Rains Become Floods* by Lurgio Galván Sánchez, *You Can Cross the Massacre On Foot* by Freddy Prestol Castillo, and *Only the Road / Solo El Camino,* an anthology of eight decades of Cuban poetry (all also published by Duke), among many other titles. Randall received the 2017 Medalla al Mérito Literario from Literatura en el Bravo, Ciudad Juárez, Mexico. In 2018 she was awarded the Poet of Two Hemispheres Prize by Poesía en Paralelo Cero in Quito, Ecuador. In 2019 she earned an honorary doctorate of letters from the University of New Mexico, and in 2022 she received the City of Albuquerque's Creative Bravo Award. Randall lives in Albuquerque with her wife of more than 37 years, the painter Barbara Byers, and travels extensively to read, lecture, and teach.

About Barbara Byers

Barbara Byers was born in Denver, Colorado, in the middle of the 20th century. She has tried to study art in formal ways but is mostly self-taught. She worked in sign shops in Denver and Albuquerque to learn that art form. She has lived in Albuquerque for 45 years, painting signs, teaching kids with special needs, and making art. Her heart home is the desert and slick rock country of the Colorado Plateau.

Of her work, she says: "As a child, I was not nurtured but forced. As an adult, I oppose force and try to learn how to nurture myself, as well as all the people around me. Starting in the Spring of 2010, I have had the opportunity and desire to turn all my working energy to art. As a painter and maker of hand-made books, I want to brighten the world around me. I want my art to be used, looked at and enjoyed every day. The process of making this art is life itself for me. I am most whole and alive when I am working. The longer I live, the less clear the distinction between art and not art becomes. I know myself best as an artist who participates on many levels in a very complex world. Kindness is a value that comes to be more and more central to my life."